Haun
~ Places ~
of
Lancashire

On the Trail of the Paranormal

Jason Karl

COUNTRYSIDE BOOKS

NEWBURY BERKSHIRE

First published 2006
© Jason Karl 2006

COUNTRYSIDE BOOKS
3 Catherine Road
Newbury, Berkshire

To view our complete range of books,
please visit us at
www.countrysidebooks.co.uk

ISBN 1 85306 986 8
EAN 978 1 85306 986 4

*To my best friend, Veronica Charles, for sharing
so many supernatural adventures with me.*

Designed by Peter Davies, Nautilus Design
Produced through MRM Associates Ltd., Reading
Typeset by Jean Cussons Typesetting, Diss, Norfolk
Printed by Borcombe Printers plc, Romsey

•Contents•

LANCASHIRE

Bolton – Burnley – Chipping – Chorley –
Clayton-le-Moors – Clitheroe – Croxteth –
Darwen – Eccleston – Foulridge – Haigh –
Hurst Green – Little Singleton – Littleborough –
Middleton – Morecambe – Nelson – Old Langho –
Oldham – Rufford – Salford – Turton – Whalley –
Worsley – Wycoller

MAP OF HAUNTED LANCASHIRE

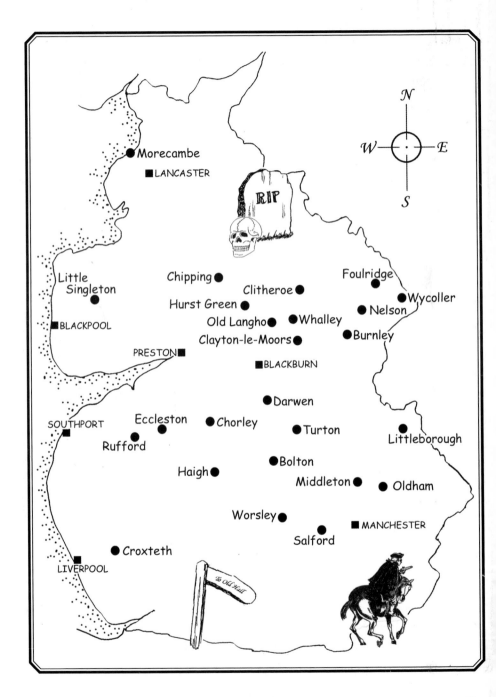

• Introduction •

I have treasured memories of Lancashire, from a very young age when my family stayed at a haunted farmhouse in Wycoller – days spent playing in fields, woods and meadows, and cosy nights tucked up in bed after ascending the dark wood panelled staircase …

Originally hailing from London, I have lived all over the country at various times in my life but I can truly say I have never felt as 'at home' as I do in Lancashire where I have lived for the past ten years. It is a proud county offering much to those who inhabit its villages, towns and cities.

For this book I have travelled far and wide throughout the area seeking known and unknown tales of ghosts and hauntings, and I am indebted to those who welcomed me and shared their, sometimes personal, stories of encounters with the world of the unexplained. Many of my investigations were in the company of a very dear friend of mine, the respected psychic medium, Veronica Charles. Veronica's affinity with the supernatural world is uncanny and she was immensely helpful to me in the preparation of this book. I have never ceased to be amazed by the accuracy of her natural talent to tune into a world that for so many of us remains unseen.

I have often been asked by colleagues from the south whether folklore and tales of the strange are more prevalent in the north, and I think that perhaps they are. There are still corners of Lancashire that appear to have been untouched by the constant onslaught of technological progress, and it is in these quiet and haunted places that I have been able to unearth a wonderful cornucopia of true tales of the beyond.

For the purposes of this book, I have used the old county boundary of Lancashire so some of the locations featured are now classed as Liverpool, Manchester or Cumbria. I have assumed that ghosts would have been unaffected by the change in 1973 and hope that true Lancastrians will appreciate my respecting the older boundaries.

Many of the locations featured are open to the public and, in these cases, I have included telephone numbers and website addresses to enable you to plan your own ghost hunting adventures. Other sites are private property and whilst I have been fortunate enough to visit these places and recount their tales here, I must ask that you respect the privacy of those who dwell in them.

I hope that this volume will entertain you, excite you and teach you something of the realm beyond that which we experience each day. I hope also that this collection will preserve forever some of the ancient and not so ancient stories that come from the haunted places of Lancashire.

If you have had an encounter with a ghost yourself, then please tell me about it by visiting my website at www.jasondexterkarl.com. Who knows, it may feature in a future publication!

Jason Karl

•Lancashire•

BOLTON
Hall i' th' Wood

Hall i' th' Wood, said to be Bolton's most haunted house.

Half hidden beneath a canopy of overhanging trees at the end of a cobbled lane, on the edge of a 1960s council estate, lurks the mysterious Hall i' th' Wood (Hall in the Wood). You would be forgiven for thinking this building does not want to be discovered. One sunny

June afternoon Veronica and I had arranged to take a tour of the building and we were about to give up our search for the place ourselves when we finally stumbled upon it. Noted as 'Bolton's most haunted house' the older timber-framed parts of the building were constructed in the 15th century by Lawrence Brownlow, whilst the more recent Jacobean stone additions grant the Hall a strange and confusing appearance, which perhaps befits a house of many hauntings.

The original structure is said to have been built to house a family of wealthy yeomen and merchants. Generations later, the building was split into several dwellings and it was in 1758 that the inventor Samuel Crompton and his family moved into rooms here. By the end of the 19th century, the manor was derelict but it was saved in 1899 by Lord Leverhulme who restored it to its former glory and presented it to the people of Bolton in memory of Samuel. It is now open to the public.

As we had arrived early, Veronica and I decided to walk around the shady grounds; it was here that Veronica first felt a brush with the unseen and described an older woman, with a wise expression, and wearing an old-fashioned headdress, peering at us from an upper window. I looked up and strained my eyes in an unsuccessful attempt to catch a glimpse of what Veronica was 'seeing' in her vision.

Veronica felt as if the woman was waiting for something, or someone. Veronica also had a separate sense of a very strong-willed man, short of stature whom she felt was in charge at the Hall. The clock struck 3 pm and we were due to meet Liz, the curator, inside. 'Did you hear that?' Veronica asked as she grabbed my arm and stopped me in my tracks, but I had heard nothing other than the sound of birdsong on the breeze. 'There was music drifting from the house, like the chords of a violin or a harp; it was only brief but I definitely heard it,' she stated. Perhaps a musical recital was in rehearsal or some background music was being played to create atmosphere for visitors, I thought, as we entered the cool flag-stoned interior.

Liz had already decided that we would begin our tour in the kitchen; here the ghost of a little old lady had been seen by several visitors. Veronica said she did not feel the room was actively haunted but she was picking up on an unhappy child who dwelt some-where in the building. Liz responded immediately, telling us that the sad spirit of a traumatised young girl is said to inhabit the attic rooms and that we would be able to visit these later in the tour. Next up was the 'Haunted Bedroom' on the first floor. As we ascended the creaking stairs I noticed that Liz was watching Veronica's reaction very closely. When we reached the top I asked Liz if the staircase had any special significance. She told me she had recently seen a very strange, solid, apparition running up it. She had only

The staircase where the footsteps were heard.

glimpsed the ankles and feet as it was running so fast. She had assumed it was a colleague but when she got to the top there was no one about. This seemed to make supernatural sense as a 'cyclical' ghost is supposed to haunt the staircase; originally a Cavalier was seen ascending the stairs although over time this haunting has decreased so that now only the sound of the footsteps is heard, or occasionally feet and legs are seen. According to records this manifesta-tion is thought to be a member of the Brownlow family who built the original house and is said to occur most frequently between Christmas Day and Twelfth Night.

Veronica had already entered the dark-panelled Brownlow Bedroom and was standing by the window. As we crossed the threshold, she told us that the woman she had seen looking out of the upper window from outside was connected to this chamber, and that in life she had paced back and forth here. I checked my notes and showed Liz the rough sketch Veronica had drawn to illustrate the headdress the ghostly watcher was wearing. Liz thought it could be that of Betty Crompton, the mother of Samuel Crompton, a previous incumbent of the Hall. There was a painting of her that matched the drawing. Several visitors over the years had refused point blank to enter the room, describing a sensation of unease, and seeing a pair of disembodied legs and feet next to the bed as they ascended the staircase outside the room. Liz then recounted an anecdote that had been related by a guest who had visited the Hall as a young child: she had watched a ghostly woman in the Brownlow Bedroom, yet none of her companions could see her. I wondered if the ghost of Betty Crompton and that of the old lady reported downstairs in the kitchen could be one and the same? However the legs, which had been described as of a distinctly male appearance, must have belonged to another phantom, which we had yet to meet.

I asked Liz if we could see the painting of Betty Crompton and she led us through several of the uneven floored chambers to the Crompton Room where the pale face of Mrs Crompton stared blankly from an aged canvas. 'That's him!' exclaimed Veronica as she pointed at another painting which turned out to be a picture of Samuel Crompton himself. Veronica declared that it was the man she had sensed before we came in. She believed he was haunting the house and that he could not leave, also that there was a great sense of unfairness associated with him. Liz told us that his ghost has been seen many times. Described as a 'small man dressed in green with a lace tunic, breeches and buckled shoes and carrying a sack over his shoulder', his angry phantom walks the rooms and corridors, finally disappearing into a wall where once a doorway existed. I realised that Veronica's description of the man 'short of stature' matched this; her feeling of 'unfairness' was also accurate, as Liz was about to reveal …

Samuel Crompton was a very talented man. As well as being an inventor, he was also an excellent mathematician, violinist and composer. Might this explain the 'chords of a violin' Veronica had heard drifting out of the Hall when we arrived? His greatest achievement was the 'Spinning Mule', an advanced loom, which he designed in 1779 and which transformed the textile industry.

Paranoid that his invention would be copied, he hid the device beneath a trapdoor in one of the rooms of the house, but his efforts were in vain and the concept was stolen; making the fortunes of many around him whilst leaving him to die in poverty at Hall i' th' Wood in 1827. It is thought that his restless ghost still wanders here in an eternal state of fury, never having reaped the rewards for his innovative work in life.

We made our way back across the upstairs landing, where the ghost of a tall man wearing a black suit and winged collar has been sighted, before deciding that the spectral emanations had weakened. I asked Liz if there were any further rooms with paranormal significance and she informed me that we had seen them all, with the exception of the attics.

Leading us through the private offices to an area not open to the public, Liz showed us a narrow dusty staircase. As we ascended in single file up into the gloom, stale air filled our lungs, and when we reached the top, we were standing in a long attic space resembling a corridor, with several areas veering off in different directions. We made our way, with some trepidation, further into the shadows and I recalled what Veronica had said earlier in the kitchen about sensing an 'unhappy child' and Liz's revelation about a traumatised young girl. 'I can hear the child now,' whispered Veronica, 'she is crying and most disturbed.' I asked Liz why she would be hidden away in the attic rooms but she didn't know, only that another medium had heard her crying hysterically. A man had also been seen striding along this corridor before disappearing. Speaking in hushed tones so as not to disturb any sensitive energies that might be around us, we crept to the end of the passage and into the room on the right. Veronica walked over to the far side of the chamber and placed her palms on the old fireplace. 'She has been punished,' she exclaimed. It was at this point that we were to touch, just for a moment, the incredible power of the spirit world. The silence was suddenly pierced by the loud and disruptive sound of feet climbing the staircase at the end of the passage and walking towards where we were standing. Liz turned as she heard the noise and I hoped that it would not destroy the potent atmosphere that had built up around us. We waited for whoever it was to appear but the footsteps ceased and no one entered the room. I looked at Liz who was as wide-eyed as myself and after glancing at my watch to note the time – 4 pm – we walked swiftly along the passage to investigate. But there was no one to be seen. Liz said it must have been a member of staff, but I knew we had just experienced a ghost!

Veronica suggested that it was time to leave the attic and, with haste, we made our way back down the staircases to the Great Hall where we questioned the staff members who were on duty that day. They declared that they hadn't left the Great Hall for the last two hours and they were the only people in the building ...

As I contemplated our peculiar experience it struck me that perhaps we had witnessed the sound of the 'striding man' that had been reported in the attics before. Was he connected in some way to the sad child spirit who according to Veronica had 'been punished'? Had we tapped into a moment of something horrific from the past that did not want to be uncovered? There is no way of knowing, but I for one shall never forget our encounter with the other side at Hall i' th' Wood.

Hall i' th' Wood
Green Way, Bolton, BL1 8UA
Telephone: 01204 332370
www.boltonmuseums.org.uk

BOLTON
SMITHILLS HALL

G rand and atmospheric, Smithills Hall dates back to the 13th century and was once owned by the ancient order of the Knights Templar. With a medieval hall at its centre, it has been altered and extended many times during its 700-year lifetime. What stands today is eclectic and sprawling, with aspects of many time periods, a strange and somewhat maze-like building that seems to never end. One-time seat of the Radcliffe family, who fought at Agincourt and in the War of the Roses (for the Lancastrians), the house was also home to the ancient Lancastrian Ainsworth family.

The 13th-century Smithills Hall, home to several ghosts.

Ghostly visitations abound here, including sightings, smells and sounds, with many encounters from recent times. The most famous ghostly tale relates to the Green Hall, a sparsely furnished chamber not always open to the public. It was here that heretical preacher George Marsh was tried for being a Protestant during the reign of Catholic Queen Mary Tudor. After being accused by Robert Barton, he was taken to Lancaster Castle to be examined further and was subsequently burned at the stake after being dowsed in tar on the orders of the Bishop of Chester in 1555, but not before he left his mark at Smithills Hall.

Legend has it that he stamped his foot in anger on a flagstone in the Green Hall where an indented footprint, which is allegedly sometimes wet to the touch, can still be seen today. It is said that the stone was removed in the 18th century and thrown into a lake but that it was quickly recovered and replaced at the Hall after alarming supernatural events began to take place. Differing opinions exist as to the validity of this tale but they cannot dismiss the many sightings of the ghost of George Marsh recorded here since 1732. His gaunt spirit, dressed in black, with dark hair, has been seen crouching by a counter in the shop area by one of the Hall guides.

Another member of staff tells of three encounters with a figure staring at her from the Pugin mirror that now hangs in the room. Was this also the spirit of Marsh? Or was it the discarnate soul of a member of the Ainsworth family who used this as a dining room whilst incumbent at the Hall? Marsh's spectre has also been seen, and sensed, in and around the staircase leading to the chamber where he was tried. One account describes an American man who revisited the building in recent years, after growing up in Bolton and coming here as a child. He recounted a memory of witnessing a man outside the Green Hall whom no one else could see. Perhaps the senses of a child are more acutely tuned to sensitive psychic vibrations? The displacement of a pair of glasses used in the museum display in the Green Hall is also blamed on the spirit of George Marsh. Often they are found thrown on the floor when staff open up in the morning.

I visited the Hall with Veronica on a hot summer's day. Upon arrival we were taken straight to the Green Hall where Veronica was immediately able to link with the energy of a strong-willed, authoritarian man. She described that something important had happened to him in this room but that it was 'out of his hands'. The spirit seemed agitated and Veronica felt that he had been responsible for scaring visitors in the past. After a couple of minutes Veronica's breathing was shallow and she became light-headed and dizzy. At this point we left the heavy psychic atmosphere of the Green Hall and made for the room known as 'The Bower'.

As part of the Tudor wing of the house, this oak-panelled room is dark with a low ceiling and is the site of another haunting at Smithills. Veronica told me that she sensed the presence of a woman here very strongly; she seemed to be a melancholy spirit wearing a 16th-century gown. Elizabeth Tatman, who was taking us around the Hall, confirmed that a spirit of that description had been reported in the area and, in particular, on the staircase that leads to the solar above. It is thought it could be the sweetheart of a man who was killed in the War of the Roses. Despite her grave demeanour this spirit seems to enjoy spooking visitors, but in a friendly fashion, for many have reported that they have felt someone pinch their behind as they ascend the staircase, even though there has been no one (living) behind them!

The chapel, which was destroyed by fire and rebuilt in 1843, is also haunted. One cold winter evening in recent years, it is recorded that a ghostly figure was seen kneeling in prayer here – a quiet and contemplative spirit which refuses to end its reflective devotions even after death. As we entered the room, Elizabeth detected a strong scent of sweet oranges, which neither Veronica nor I noticed. She was so struck by this strange occurrence that she insisted on smelling Veronica's perfume to see if it was the same aroma – it wasn't! Veronica sensed unhappiness in the room; could this be explained by the wandering soul that has been seen here, or by the people who, in the past, were forced to come and worship here against their will?

There are plenty more ghosts at the Hall, many as yet unidentified. When the building was in use as a retirement home, elderly residents regularly reported hearing the psychic echo of galloping horses. Shuffling footsteps both inside and on the gravel outside have also been heard. A Victorian maid has been glimpsed, going about her business before disappearing, and a strange perfume thought to belong to the spirit of someone named 'Isabella' haunts Mrs Ainsworth's withdrawing room. Records of a phantom cat date back over 70 years when it was said to have been responsible for scratching people's faces whilst they slept, but the most recent ghosts are two children playing – their voices, footsteps and laughter echoing through the deserted parts of the house to this day – the final members of the spectral family at Smithills Hall.

Smithills Hall
Smithills Dean Road, Bolton, BL1 7NP
Telephone: 01204 332377
www.smithills.co.uk

BURNLEY
TOWNELEY HALL

Towneley Hall, where the sound of marching boots has been heard on the driveway.

This 14th-century fortified house was the one-time haunt of the Towneley family, whose warrior exploits have been chronicled since the early 13th century. With an abundance of paranormal anecdotes recorded in the archives, it is not surprising that it is now generally accepted that some members of the family haunt there still …

Top of the Hall's hauntings is the classic Tudor ghost; this time of the late Sir John Towneley. An undisputed vagabond in life, his wraith is doomed to walk the passageways of the house and among the densely wooded grounds for all eternity; a deserved punishment for cruelly turning peasants out of their homes to acquire more land in his tyrannical pursuit of wealth and power during life. As befits his crime, this reckless Tudor lord was to profit little from his escapade and is now locked in a state of perpetual torment; time a plenty to explore his tortured conscience.

A rather happier shade is our second spirit at historic Towneley, that of the 'White Lady' whose identity remains unknown. She has been seen flitting among the trees and emerging from the woods and gliding towards a small stone bridge where she disappears. One night, many years ago, two local teenagers decided to see if they could see the ghost and, as midnight approached, they climbed over a wall and began to explore the grounds in darkness. What they experienced was not the ghost of the White Lady but the psychic echo of the Hall's third acknowledged haunting. As they neared the house the distinct sound of marching boots on the driveway was heard but, as they emerged from the undergrowth, the sound ceased and there was nothing to be seen. It is thought that this strange phenomenon is the result of the march of Oliver Cromwell's soldiers who were ordered to arrest Charles Towneley, a Royalist sympathiser, over 350 years ago.

Other sundry sightings include a wandering light moving from window to window, espied from the Hall's exterior in the dead of night. Conspiratorial whisperings have been heard on the Long Gallery, accompanied by a chilling freeze and disembodied footsteps where no mortal walks.

When Veronica and I visited, we were welcomed to the house by curator Ken Darwen. We began our tour in the Regency dining room. 'I want to dance,' said Veronica as we entered the elaborately decorated chamber. 'People are used to dancing here,' she continued. Apart from replying 'That's interesting', Ken said no more as he led us into the room next door, which was devoid of furniture and set up ready for a wedding. Sumptuously decorated, with rich red drapes at the windows and a sparkling crystal chandelier, it was easy to picture scenes that must have taken place here in times past. Veronica sensed the presence of an elderly lady wearing a rigid Victorian dress, with pearls around her neck and a large silver locket. She identified her as a member of the Towneley family and felt she was a very domineering personality. In fact, the wraith told Veronica that the servants were scared of her.

Turning to Ken, I asked if he could identify this spirit. He said that the description matched that of Alice O'Hagan who was the last private resident of the Hall and died in 1921. She was a very strong entrepreneur, an independent thinker and staunch supporter of women's causes. Veronica also said that the room had a sense of singing, theatre and music about it. Ken confirmed that it was known as the Music Room since in centuries long gone this was the place where musical entertainment and dancing would take place.

After leaving the luxurious Regency rooms, we climbed the austere wooden staircase to the top floor and emerged onto the gloomy and deserted,

The Music Room, haunted by a member of the Towneley family.

Elizabethan Long Gallery. Here Veronica sensed the presence of a lady in Edwardian dress, carrying a fan, and wearing a powdered wig. She described her as having a pale face, as if she was wearing white powder of some kind. Knowing that a White Lady was supposed to haunt the grounds and woods, I asked Ken if he knew of any sightings of this ghost within the house. Ken confirmed that she had been reported floating silently along the Long Gallery many times and that some people have seen her looking out of the windows.

We made our way across the creaking floorboards of the gallery and into the Elizabethan bedchamber. Here Veronica found our next spectre, but this one was doing its best to remain hidden. 'There is a man here; he keeps appearing and disappearing in my vision. It is confusing me as I feel he is connected very strongly with this area, yet I cannot tell exactly where. I glimpsed him first in the gallery and he went into this room but now he has disappeared again. He has long hair and is very straight-laced. There is a definite religious connection, a Catholic connection, and I keep seeing a staircase, but not the one we came up – this one is much smaller.' Unable to see another staircase in the room, we rejoined Ken on the Long Gallery where I asked him if there were any other steps in the vicinity. 'There is the secret staircase,' he said, leading us to a section of wood panelling, which he opened to reveal a small spiral staircase leading down into the bowels of the house below. 'That's it!' exclaimed Veronica. 'There are secrets here, secrets that need to be kept. Is there a religious connection with this staircase?' Ken nodded and told us that the steps led down to a chapel far below.

Deciding that we must visit the chapel, but voting against using the secret stairs, we replaced the panelling and made our way down the main stairs, eventually arriving at the chapel. Ken explained that the entire room had been moved from another location in the house, piece by piece, in 1736, and pains-takingly restored in every detail in this new location. 'There are no spirits in this room, but I do see a Mother Superior – she is praying,' said Veronica. 'Well the altarpiece that you see here was removed and taken to a convent in the late 19th century before being returned here in 1969,' Ken told us. This seemed to fit in with Veronica's psychic impression. The room does have a peculiar anecdote connected with it: apparently a human head was stored in a concealed cupboard in the wall until the 1940s when it was removed and buried. Veronica tried to sense something about the disembodied relic but because it had been removed so long ago she was unable to pick up any trace of it.

Next on the tour were the attics; previously used as servants' quarters, they are now storage areas for unwanted furniture, paintings and antiques from the Hall. Entering what Ken called the Archive Room, Veronica sensed two women. The first she described as having a disfigured face, the consequences of an accident with a hot iron. The second was a talkative lady in dark simple attire, with shoulder-length, dark brown hair. She told Veronica that she had been a servant in the house during the 1800s and she had experienced much sorrow after becoming pregnant with an illegitimate child, which she had lost as a result of a miscarriage.

We descended back into the main house and Ken led us through the kitchen and into the servants' dining room where we met Christine Howard, a guide who has had a few ghostly encounters herself. She told me that one winter several years ago, she observed three spirits: a man, a woman and a dog. They were hazy and indistinct shapes and they melted away after a few moments. I asked her if working at the haunted Hall scared her, to which she replied, 'Definitely not, I have a psychic intuition myself and my husband is an undertaker'. She has also seen another spectral inhabitant of the building, this time a maid wearing a mob-cap and apron. 'It was during the winter season in 2004 and I noticed a figure walking through the servants' hall. I followed her calling out "We're closing now" but she disappeared around a corner and when I turned she was nowhere to be seen.' I wondered if Veronica would sense this serving spectre but she was more interested in the adjoining room.

Christine and I followed her as she walked through, until she almost collapsed and shouted out 'My leg!' and I stepped forward to stop her from falling to the ground. Christine started laughing, which seemed extremely inappropriate, but quickly explained herself by saying she knew why it had happened. Puzzled we looked around the room for a clue but saw nothing other than a series of glass cases showcasing artefacts from all over the world, many of them Egyptian. Christine pointed to a large sarcophagus to Veronica's left, inlaid with a bright blue scarab, and said, 'He's only got one leg, that's why you nearly fell over!' We stared in amazement as Christine elaborated, telling us that Lady O' Hagan – whom Veronica identified as the spirit in the Music Room earlier on – had been a great collector of Egyptian relics and that the mummy in the sarcophagus had been analysed and was missing half of its left leg from the knee down!

As we thanked Ken and Christine and left behind the house of many hauntings and the Egyptian with one leg, I turned to Veronica and asked her if she had ever been affected by something as strange in the past. 'I am never surprised by the spirit world,' she replied. 'Having been blessed, or cursed depending which way you look at it, since I was a child, I sense things I want to, and things I don't. But a connection with a crumbling Egyptian, now that's a first – even for me!'

Towneley Hall
Burnley, BB11 3RQ
Telephone: 01282 424213
www.towneleyhall.org.uk

CHIPPING
THE SUN INN

The sad story of a lovelorn ghost is often retold around a crackling fire in the inn on the hill in the remote village of Chipping – sometimes referred to as 'Chilling Chipping' as the ghosts are said to outnumber the living. Here, in this picturesque yet desolate place, the Sun Inn on Windy Street hides the phantom of local celebrity spectre, Elizabeth Dean.

During the 1800s Elizabeth worked as a servant at the inn. As she was only just 20 and had a face to tempt any man, it is not surprising to learn that Lizzie, as she was known, caught the attention of a member of the local gentry. Encouraged by his dashing looks, quick wit and charm she soon began a passionate secret love affair with him, but he was not to be trusted …

The Sun Inn stands opposite the church in the village of Chipping.

Lizzie watched as time went by and one young village girl after another was happily wed to her betrothed in the church opposite the inn. She hoped desperately that one day she would stand at the altar as a bride herself; a promise made to her by her clandestine lover. But this tale has a cruel twist for, upon a sunny November morning in 1835, whilst watching the church from her attic bedroom, she was witness to a terrible scene. As she looked closer her heart filled with dread as she spied her beloved laughing with another woman – his new bride! Lizzie was heartbroken and distraught.

In a tragic fit of despair she strung herself up by a rafter, kicking the chair from beneath her feet and shouting a deadly curse that was to reverberate through time for centuries to come. 'I curse you by all things good and true, your offspring mute, and their children too,' and with that her tormented soul was bound forever to the building where she had once loved … and lost.

The story has it that the curse of Lizzie Dean came to pass, with the descendants of the bride who took her place born mute, as were their children, and their children's children. Although this cannot be historically verified, it is an undisputed fact that her ghost haunts the inn to this day and she has been seen by landlords and locals alike, wandering the passages in search of peace and perhaps her deceitful lover.

When I first met Steve and Jeanne who manage the inn, they didn't hesitate in telling me of the numerous encounters they have had with the ghost. Steve had seen her with his own eyes on no fewer than six occasions. He described her as a friendly presence which took on two distinctly different appearances; either dressed in the garb of a serving maid with a black dress, white apron and hood, or else manifesting as a black, solid, shadowy figure without features. He and Jeanne had heard her opening and closing doors with some force and even witnessed a curious scent of lavender in the main bar, which was attributed to her as it was pungent and inexplicably arrived with a cold chill – several customers also witnessed this. But the sightings and her voice were harder to understand. When he had seen her she was either walking in from the front door towards the back door or moving towards the staircase up to the first floor. Every time she had been as solid as a living person, not wispy or transparent in any way. She had also called his name when he had been cleaning the beer lines in the cellars, which he usually did every Friday morning. Twice he had heard a female voice calling 'Steve' even though there had been no one around and the place was closed to customers.

Barman Simon added to the story, telling me that, shortly after he had started his job, he was in the cellar cleaning the beer lines as Steve had been busy elsewhere, when he too heard his name called by a female who, when he investigated, could not be found. On a separate occasion Simon reported seeing a figure walk out of the lobby door, past the bar and out of the front door. Seconds later he ran out of the pub to see who it was but found no one to account for what he had witnessed.

Several journalists have reported strange encounters in the building. One saw what he described as a 'period figure dressed as a maid' walking towards the front door as he sat quietly eating lunch one day. Another, from a major magazine, accompanied me on my first full night investigation at the inn in 2000. On this occasion, although no one actually saw the ghost of Lizzie Dean, her presence was strongly felt by the journalist who wrote very movingly of the experience. Later the same evening one of my team measured a high reading of anomalous (abnormal) electromagnetic activity, often associated with the presence of a spirit, near the main bar at 12.43 am – the very area where the ghost makes its most regular appearances.

Another journalist, and her sceptical photographer, this time from the *Daily Mail*, accompanied Veronica and myself around the inn one blustery day in November 2003. Veronica was drawn immediately to the front door area where she reported 'a great sense of sadness, a spirit who has lost everything'. We then climbed the creaking spiral staircase towards the attic room where the investigation continued with Veronica proclaiming: 'The spirit is that of a woman who looks older than her years. She says her name is known and she has no interest in talking to me. I feel she may be more at ease with a male psychic, perhaps she has appeared more to men than women.'

Veronica was correct. In most cases the ghost has indeed been reported by men. However, Jeanne, Steve's wife, also encountered Lizzie's spirit one early morning when she went downstairs to unlock the doors for the cleaner. She opened the first door into the porch at approximately 8.55 am but was distracted by the sound of the voice of a young girl. She was unable to discern what she was saying but she had the impression she was muttering to herself – not speaking to someone else. She assumed it was the cleaner who had decided to use the back door instead of the front but when she opened that door there was no one to be seen.

The female journalist and her male photographer were not fortunate enough to see the ghost during our visit but they came away believing they had experienced something of the building's haunted past. During a dowsing experiment in which they attempted to locate paranormal energies by the use of metallic rods, they had both, without knowing, highlighted the rafter where Lizzie committed suicide.

Giving further credence to the spirit's predilection for males, I was told of the time when a group of male senior citizens was playing a game of snooker in the upper pool room, which lies above the main bar and leads to the attic bedroom. The men described how suddenly a figure of a woman dressed as a maid had

The grave of Lizzie Dean.

walked through the room, passed the snooker table and headed down the staircase for the bar areas. Several members of the group rushed after her, bursting into the main bar and demanding if anyone there had seen her. But, as is usual in these circumstances, she had not been sighted by those drinking below.

In July 2000 the village held a pageant, the highlight of which was to be a re-enactment of the story of Lizzie Dean's demise, but on the Monday prior to the event Jeanne was met by several excited children who had knocked on her door to tell her that the window of Lizzie's attic bedroom was wide open. The room is rarely used and had not been entered for several years. After unlocking the room to investigate, Jeanne found that there were no visible signs of the window having being opened by human hands; the floor of the room was caked in dust and there were no footprints. Coupled with the fact that considerable force is required to open the window, Jeanne concluded that Lizzie was showing her approval of the pageant, which proceeded the following Saturday as planned.

I have been lucky enough to investigate this haunted pub on four occasions over the last few years and have taken several different mediums on various occasions to try and ascertain more evidence for the haunting. In 2002 I was amazed when I set a challenge to two mediums to locate the grave of Lizzie Dean in darkness when neither had any prior knowledge of the story. They both went straight to the gravestone, which stands to the right of the church, hidden beneath a canopy of trees which is inscribed with a heartfelt epitaph:

Sacred to the Memory of Elizabeth Dean who departed this life November 5th 1835 in the 20th year of her age. There is a hallowed sweetness in cherishing a remembrance of those we loved.

The Sun Inn
Windy Street, Chipping, Forest of Bowland PR3 2GD
Telephone: 01995 61206

CHORLEY
ASTLEY HALL

The stuccoed Elizabethan façade of Astley Hall at Chorley belies its true origin, which dates back to the Tudor era when Robert Charnock became the first inhabitant of the building. Since 1922 this noted haunted manor has been owned and operated by the local council who run guided ghost tours in the winter months; and they have plenty of material.

One overcast and rainy day I paid a visit to the manor in the company of psychic medium, Sybil Lucas-Brewer. As we entered the building, which was unusually devoid of other visitors, it was as if we were stepping back in time. I had already received reports that the warden, Carole Fox, had endured an unsettling sighting not long before. She described walking into the kitchen one day and seeing a woman in a roped off area by the fireplace. She was about to tell her that she wasn't allowed there when she noticed she was wearing a Victorian dress. Carole was terrified and ran out of the room. Along with other staff, Carole has also heard ghostly footsteps, laughter and music coming from empty rooms and once saw a little girl who disappeared into a row of chairs.

Astley Hall, © Lancashire County Council.

Intrigued by Carole's experiences, I asked Sybil if she could follow in the footsteps of the phantoms that haunt the Hall and elaborate further. As we entered the elegant 18th-century drawing room, its walls adorned with fraying tapestries, Sybil's mood turned sombre. She said there was a strong memory of a funeral wake lingering from the past. She could see several ladies dressed in black, but no one was speaking.

As we passed into the kitchen in the 16th-century section of the building, Sybil became aware of the presence of distinctly separate female entities. She mentioned the names Alice and Mary-Marie. I tried to locate these names on the historical family trees associated with the incumbents of the Hall but was unable to trace them. However, if the spirit or spirits haunting the kitchen were servants as opposed to gentry, then their names would not appear on the family trees.

In the courtyard Sybil described 'frantic activity of children, people and horses', which was interesting as that part of the house used to be quite different from what can be seen nowadays. In centuries past this was the servants' access area for the dairy, game larder, sleeping quarters and dining room. It is also the place where the water supply for the building was pumped. Naturally this would have been a constant hive of activity in the building's heyday as a grand house.

There were other shadows of a spectral nature lingering faintly among the lavish interiors. Amongst them was a country gent wearing a red waistcoat warming himself by the fireplace in the Great Hall who 'gestured to welcome us into the room', according to Sybil. Later I discovered that this ghost has been seen entering the house and walking up the main staircase, on many occasions accompanied by a child. It is thought to be the ghost of Reginald Tatton who was the last private owner of the Hall. So 'normal' has this sighting become that guides no longer take much notice. Sybil also 'saw' a woman excitedly awaiting the arrival of her beau in the Towneley-Parker room and a child riding a hobby horse in the Long Gallery – could this have been the girl who has been seen accompanying Reginald in the Great Hall?

The ghosts of Astley Hall all seem to be benevolent spirits of a bygone age, each connected with a different aspect of this house of memories.

Astley Hall
Astley Park, off Hall Gate, Chorley, PR7 1NP
Telephone: 01257 262166

CLAYTON-LE-MOORS
THE DUNKENHALGH HOTEL

Dating back to 1285, the grand Gothic pile known as Dunkenhalgh in Clayton-le-Moors, is now a luxury hotel. It was home to the Rishton family until 1571 when it passed to Thomas Walmesley, an accomplished man of the law who became Member of Parliament for

Lancashire in 1589. Later it passed to the Petre family who inhabited the building until the Second World War. It is from the time of the Petres' incumbency that the tale of the Dunkley bogart originates. Within living memory, fear of the bogart, or ghost, was so strong that many would not pass by the building after nightfall on Christmas Eve, for that is when the spirit is fated to return to its old haunt.

Legend has it that some time in the 18th century a French governess named Lucette was taken into service, to care for the children of the family. She was a beautiful young woman who, after being introduced to a dashing young officer staying with the family one Christmastide, fell madly in love. The story relates that he abandoned her soon after they had consummated their relationship, promising that he would return in the New Year, when they would be married. But it was not to be. Accounts of the tale differ in their opinion: some say he never intended to return, others state that he was delayed against his own will. Either way the sad Lucette was left to cope with a pregnancy out of wedlock, a situation of deep shame at that time.

The Petres were said to be sympathetic to begin with but as her predicament became more obvious and the older servants began to treat Lucette with disdain, it became apparent that she could not stay under the same roof. Unable to return to her family in France, she became desperate. One stormy night she took her own life by jumping off a small stone bridge into the swollen waters of the River Hyndburn, which flows through the grounds of the mansion. Her bloated corpse was pulled from the reeds downstream the following morning and she was buried in an unmarked grave. This tale has a second terrible twist, which says that Lucette's lover returned soon afterwards but, alas, was too late to save his young bride to be and he died after in a duel with Lucette's brother, who had been sent from France to avenge her untimely demise.

Her mournful ghost, eternally lost in a loveless time warp, still walks the halls, passageways and grounds where she found earthly love. Most commonly her ghost is seen on Christmas Eve, near the site of the old stone bridge, where she flung herself into oblivion all those years ago.

I took Veronica to the Dunkenhalgh Hotel to see if she would be able to pick up any traces of the sad spirit of Lucette, or indeed find any other spectral memories of the past lingering in its environs. As we approached the entrance, Veronica slipped into a trance-like state, attuning herself to the vibrations of the spirit world. We were directed past a striking staircase and into the ornately-decorated Dunklaw Room. Veronica became aware of a woman rushing down the staircase and dashing into the room. She described her as around 35 years of age, wearing a tight corset, with a pale blue dress, and carrying a fan. She appeared to Veronica to be a servant, yet there was a strong feeling that she commanded respect in the house.

It was at this point Veronica was getting out of breath and said she felt a rush of cold pass through her. I asked her to sever the link with this spirit – which she did. But she wasn't finished yet. She sensed also a male entity linked to this room although he was much fainter and from a different era. He was connected to the fireplace and seemed to be casting judgment.

It was at this point that I noticed a man standing in the corner of the room watching us. When I caught his eye he introduced himself as Robert Gregg and explained that he had worked in the building as concierge for many years. When I enquired what he had thought of Veronica's evidence, he turned to her and explained that everything she said was just right: the ghost of Lucette had been described with great accuracy. To illustrate his point he led us into the Oak Room where an old painting of a beautiful woman hangs on the wall. She is wearing a pale-coloured dress and smiling out of the canvas, and I was not surprised to see that she holds a fan – exactly as Veronica had said. The painting has an uncanny way of appearing to stare at you wherever you stand in the room. Robert then told us that her ghost is often associated with inexplicable cold draughts and appears suddenly, striking fear into those unfortunate enough to see it.

He recounted the time during Christmas 2003 when the banqueting manager had an encounter that caused him to resign forthwith. The manager was an ex Royal Air Force officer and not the kind of person who would be scared easily; but he had described how, whilst in the Pendle Suite, he had experienced a force 'dancing and swirling around him' accompanied by a chilling cold that penetrated right into his very being. Apparently this stayed with him for some time and he left three days later, never to return.

Robert also told us that during 2000 a grand old lady had come to the hotel with her family to celebrate her 90th birthday. It transpired that, as a young girl, she had played in the house and clearly remembered the ghost of Lucette, but also another spirit, this time of a man who appeared in a hideous skeletal form. Robert then took us into yet another magnificent chamber where many portraits of noted dignitaries lined the lime-washed plaster. Straining her eyes to see a painting on the other side of the room more clearly, Veronica recognised the figure as the ghost in the Dunklaw Room. Robert nodded with satisfaction and revealed that the painting was of Judge Walmsley who did indeed cast his judgements in the very room where Veronica had 'seen' him by the fireplace.

Spurred on by success and with a creeping sense of sadness for the forlorn spirit of Lucette, we ventured into the gardens where our next discovery was revealed amongst overgrown briars and tangled vines. Robert described how, on Christmas Day in 2002, a dark storm raged above the hotel and a powerful bolt of lightning struck an ancient oak tree and brought it hurtling to the ground just yards from the stone bridge where Lucette met her tragic end. When the storm passed, an ancient ritual totem was uncovered, hidden for many years within the roots of the very tree itself. It was a stone obelisk, hand-carved with Celtic symbols on each side. Amazed by the discovery Robert had informed hotel staff of the curious find, but with the Christmas season underway he decided to forget about it until the end of the festivities. That was a mistake as shortly afterwards the obelisk was stolen and has never been recovered. So what was this strange artefact? And why was it hidden beneath an oak tree? Could this be an indication of ancient pagan magic having taken place on the land here, or was it a Victorian whimsy, simply lost and forgotten?

Layers of history and mystery abound at the Dunkenhalgh, with the sad spirit of a beautiful French governess, the spectre of a judge and a fallen oak tree whose story may never be known.

The Dunkenhalgh Hotel
Clayton-le-Moors, Accrington, BB5 5JP
Telephone: 01254 303450
www.macdonaldhotels.co.uk/dunkenhalgh

CLITHEROE
BROWSHOLME HALL

Browsholme Hall, © Lancashire County Council.

T he country seat of the Parker family, Browsholme Hall, is a mix of Tudor and Elizabethan architecture which houses a remarkable collection of antiquarian portraits, Regency furniture, and arms and armour. Nestling deep in the Forest of Bowland, it is still very much a family home and I was delighted to be invited to investigate the ghostly goings-on in this grand mansion by the current owner, Mr Robert Redmayne Parker.

Accompanied by Veronica, I explored the dark oak panelled rooms on the ground floor in search of signs of the supernormal. But traces of any spirits were at best weak and, apart from the hint of a Cavalier in the Ante Room and a small Oriental gentleman in the Library, which Veronica thought was connected with the *objets d' art* as opposed to the Hall itself, there was little to be found.

However, at the end of our visit, Mr Parker told us of hauntings in other parts of the property, to which we had not been granted access. The first tale concerns a 'Screaming Skull' which is kept in a cupboard under lock and key and is never shown to anyone other than male heirs of the Parker family. Legend has it that if it is removed from the house all manner of unpleasant macabre activity will occur. The origin of the skull is unknown but it is thought to be that of a female and records do indicate that it has been known to have caused trouble of a paranormal nature in the past. Mr Parker told me that, at the end of the 19th century, an ancestor of his decided to rid Browsholme Hall of its creepy relic and removed the skull, quickly returning it only days later after a flurry of strange activity broke out there. After informing me that he himself did not believe in any tales of the supernatural, Mr Parker refused to show me the skull, despite my fervent request and willingness to accept the consequences.

The second ghostly encounter at Browsholme concerns the curious tale of a dare from centuries ago. The challenge was to ride a white horse up the interior staircase and although legend has it that the rider survived to tell the tale his steed was not so lucky and can now be seen perpetually galloping up the staircase in phantom form. A painting of a white horse hangs halfway up the stairs commemorating the story and it is said that if it should fall off the wall a member of the family will soon die. In an attempt to thwart the powers of the supernatural and prevent the curse ever being fulfilled Mr Parker has securely screwed the painting firmly to the wall to ensure there is no possibility of it ever falling.

The last ghost of Browsholme lurks in a cottage in the grounds of the Hall. Said to be the ghost of a former gamekeeper who committed suicide by hanging, this miserable shade allegedly haunts his former home, tormenting those that he left behind.

Browsholme Hall
Clitheroe, BB5 3DE
Telephone: 01254 827160
www.browsholme.co.uk

CLITHEROE
THE INN AT WHITEWELL

T he spectacular setting of the Inn at Whitewell, deep within a wooded valley at Dunsop Bridge, near Clitheroe, is one of the reasons why thousands of tourists flock to the Forest of Bowland each and every year, but what most of them won't realise as they tuck into hearty meals and ale at this historic inn, is that it houses more than just spirits of the bottled kind.

The building which exists today was largely built in 1818 but remnants of the earlier dwelling can still be seen. The inn is now a successful luxury hotel and restaurant managed by Charlie Bowman, whose family has lived in the building for the last 30 years. Charlie offered to take Veronica and myself on a tour of the hotel and so, without further ado, we ascended the staircase and entered the first bedroom – Room 8.

Charlie told me that as a child he had used this room as his bedroom but that he had never seen or felt anything strange or ghostly there. However, Veronica described seeing a woman standing in the room, a slender lady with a blue ribbon and pearl necklace, probably in her mid thirties who had a connection with books. Charlie then went on to tell us that in the mid 1980s a houseguest had

Room 8 from where a ghost stares out of the window.

slept in his room and the following morning reported seeing the apparition of a woman standing by the window. Charlie's mother believed she saw the same ghost several times during the following week, but from the outside of the building, staring at her out of the window in Room 8.

We left the haunted bedroom behind and made our way back downstairs to the public bars. It was here that Veronica sensed another presence – this time a man named Jack, an old regular who used to drink at the inn and who was associated with horses in the area immediately outside the inn. He may have lived off the land and been involved in organised poaching. She felt drawn particularly to the end of the building now painted white. Charlie explained that at one time there were stables on the site and that centuries ago the area outside had been used as the main market for the surrounding villages.

Could Jack have planned his poaching pursuits with cohorts at the market? Strangely enough the white painted cottage section of the inn was once the keeper's cottage – maybe it was Jack's?

The Inn at Whitewell.
Near Clitheroe, Lancashire. BB7 3AT
01200 448222

CROXTETH
CROXTETH HALL

Described as the finest working country estate in the North-West, Tudor Croxteth Hall stands proudly amid Victorian landscaped gardens in a 500-acre country park. Once the grandiose home of the Molyneux family, the Earls of Sefton, who built the Hall in 1575 and retained ownership for generations, it was bequeathed to the City of Liverpool in 1972 when the last earl passed away. The house had been rebuilt in 1702 and extended in 1902, leaving the impressive Edwardian wing that is now accepted as the 'front' of the building. Therefore, the mansion that survives today is a magnificent example of forgotten decadent times.

Tales of hauntings go hand in hand with old houses and Croxteth has its fair share of ghostly reminders of a long lost past. I was invited to visit the Hall by Neil Bascombe who works for Liverpool Council. So, accompanied by Veronica, I arrived on a cold autumn afternoon when the building was closed to the public to try and uncover some of the mansion's mysteries.

Our first port of call was at the home of Raymond and Elda Lempereur who live in a grace and favour flat in the grounds of the Hall. They had worked as chef to Lady Sefton and chef's assistant respectively for 24 years, and I had been told that the Lempereurs had several stories to tell.

We were delighted to receive a warm welcome from them and lost no time in getting down to business. Elda recalled how one afternoon soon after arriving at the Hall she had needed to see Grace, the housekeeper, and so set about the house to find her. After searching the ground and first floor she assumed she must be in the private quarters on the second floor so she climbed the staircase to the corridor known as the Sefton Passage. As she neared the top she heard some voices and thought she had found her but when she turned into the corridor there was no one to be seen. By now the voices were louder, but still peculiarly indistinct, like whisperings from no particular direction. So Elda called out, at which point the voices stopped, just as if they had been switched off. It was deathly silent and so Elda continued to the other end of the corridor where the whisperings once again became apparent. She called out once more but received no response, so assumed that the housekeeper did not wish to be disturbed and was in one of the rooms nearby. Elda then went quietly back downstairs.

Later on that afternoon, she bumped into Grace in the kitchen and apologised for disturbing her earlier. Bemused by the comment Grace explained that she had been out of the house all afternoon and therefore Elda must have heard the ghost. She went on to tell Elda that three of the housemaids had also heard voices, seen strange shadows and experienced a creeping cold in that area of the Hall.

I asked Elda if she considered herself to be psychic. She replied that she believed she had some sensitivity, as she had once experienced a strange sighting of a staircase that had long since been removed at an old church in

France. She had also heard children's voices in the flat where she lived whilst her grandchild was staying. It was as if two children were whispering in the corner of the room, but it ceased as soon as her grandchild went home.

It was now Raymond's turn to share his ghostly tales and he began by telling me he did not believe in such things but he had seen a soldier dressed in a blue 1914 uniform and helmet near the Gothic porch at the side of the Hall. At the time he dismissed it as an hallucination but added that perhaps it was something more as the head gardener, Arthur Dallas, had witnessed a whole scene of apparitions in the same place. It was a dark misty night when Arthur was returning from the village to his home in the grounds. As he made his way up the drive and past the side of the house he was surprised to see a line of soldiers wearing red tunics and armed with guns, which they were aiming at the Hall. Alarmed by their stance and knowing they should not be there he shouted out but at this point they swiftly disappeared into the rolling mist.

Other staff have also had encounters with those from the beyond at Croxteth. A young security guard making his rounds on the first evening of his employment experienced a strange feeling on the staircase to the Sefton Passage and was unable to persuade his dogs to enter the corridor – spooked by his encounter he left the very next day! Another account tells of a typist who froze with fear as her office became icy cold and a shadowy figure moved quickly across the room.

The Sefton Passage, where ghostly voices are heard.

Another employee at the Hall received an unwelcome fright during October 2005 when a team of ghost hunters was conducting a séance in the building. Dave Palmer is reported to have heard the voice of the late butler who died in 1991 after serving at the Hall since 1945.

One common phenomenon reported in haunted houses is that of spectral scents and Croxteth has its own variation – the smell of baking bread. It wafts through the empty rooms even though the bread oven has long since been removed. Could this strange occurrence be associated with the phantasm of a blond girl who has been seen working with a rolling pin in the former confectionery next to the kitchen? Another member of staff, Rita Jackson, said that she has often felt as if she was being watched from the corner of the kitchen and now refuses to work there alone.

It was now time to see what Veronica could sense in the Hall itself and so, as the last rays of sun shone on the elaborate Edwardian façade of the house, we entered the gloomy wooden panelled interior, beginning our tour in the old Dining Room.

As we entered I noticed that Veronica's demeanour changed. She had been buoyant as we had made our way there but her face now told a different story. I could see she was uncomfortable. She sensed a very powerful man dressed in a black bow tie and dinner suit, carrying a pocket watch. He had short ginger hair and a neatly clipped moustache and Veronica felt he was in torment. She added that there was a possible suicide connection and that the man might have been rather too fond of the drink. Clearly ill at ease with the presence of this lingering shade, Veronica asked to move on, so we left the old Dining Room and its ghostly incumbent behind.

Navigating our way through a variety of maze-like passageways and dilapidated chambers we strolled through the 210-roomed mansion, eventually arriving at the Billiard Room. Veronica experienced a strong scent of tobacco here although I could detect nothing. Neil confirmed that the smell had been reported many times by both staff and customers, who have been unable to find a logical explanation for the pungent aroma. As the room is heavy with atmosphere and dressed with wax manikins it is easy to understand why people often comment that it feels 'spooky', but we were yet to visit the most haunted room in the Hall.

The chamber ominously known as 'Bedroom O' lies along a dusty corridor, far beyond the reach of the public and behind a locked door. Veronica bravely entered the room first, the heavily-draped windows casting long shadows across the floor in the last afternoon sun. She described a delicate woman aged around 35 who suffered an early demise from tuberculosis. Veronica said that this woman was the cause of cold spots around the building. Attended by maids, she was sometimes carried around in something that resembled a sedan chair although her spirit was very strong here and this may have been the room where she crossed over to the spirit world. She was a travelled lady of means, a lover of music and had a beautiful singing voice. As her spectre faded from Veronica's view she was humming a merry tune.

I wondered if Neil could identify this musical spectre, but the history of the Hall is sketchy and there have been so many generations of inhabitants and guests there that her identity is not immediately apparent. It did occur to me in hindsight that maybe the whisperings heard by Elda and the housemaids in this area of the Hall were, in fact, the psychic echo of voices of the maids attending this poor soul on her deathbed.

As we drove away from Croxteth Hall and its army of sentient and non sentient inhabitants behind, I realised we had not come any nearer to solving the mystery of who haunts the mansion. In fact, we had added even more unknown wraiths to an ever-increasing spectral population.

Croxteth Hall
Croxteth Hall & Country Park, Liverpool, L12 0HB
Telephone: 0151 233 6910
www.croxteth.co.uk

DARWEN
MARLEY'S WINE BAR

I was introduced to the hauntings at Marley's Wine Bar by Kerri Richards – a good friend of mine who used to work behind the bar at the club. When she started working at Marley's, she met Vicky Davies who told her that the three-storey building was known for being haunted and, on several occasions,

The haunted wine bar.

glasses had jumped off the shelves behind the bar and landed unbroken on the floor.

It was not long after this that Kerri first witnessed a supernatural incident in the building. The wall lights in the upstairs bar were dimming and brightening and she assumed someone was fiddling with the dimmer switch, as this was the only way to make them behave in that fashion. Kerri called Vicky and told her someone must be messing around upstairs but, when she went up, there was no one to be seen, only a few customers so engrossed in conversation they had not even noticed the lights behaving in this odd fashion. Vicky and Kerri were the only staff on site at the time.

Vicky had always felt uncomfortable when she had cause to go to the top floor flat where the valuable drinks were stored. On several occasions she had experienced the sensation of being 'watched', and, for no apparent reason, she decided to nickname the ghost 'Frank'. When I interviewed her she told me that the building used to be an Italian restaurant and that some previous staff members had once come in for a drink and asked if she had met the ghost. Apparently the building had been haunted for many years.

One night Vicky was locking up, accompanied by another staff member whose boyfriend was waiting patiently for them next to the bar. A side door was open and, as the boyfriend glanced down the stairs beyond, he watched a 'white misty form' move quickly down the stairs and disappear. Evidently he refused point blank to ever enter the premises again!

I decided to spend a night investigating the haunted winebar and so I assembled a group of investigators from the Ghost Research Foundation, along with psychic Angela Borrows. The vigil began by taking baseline readings of electromagnetic energy, temperatures and sound, but it wasn't until the early hours of the morning that anything strange happened. 'It began with a sound like a triangle being played,' recalled Angela. Several members of the team heard this on two occasions and described it as mellow twinkling music, perhaps that of a lullaby. Later, two male voices were heard talking by Vicky and Angela. Both girls were a little shaken by the experience and, soon after, a fleeting dark shadow was glimpsed moving across a wall, but the highlight of the investigation occurred when we found a high reading of electromagnetic energy which could not be explained. The anomaly was localised and appeared to 'move' around, before 'running' between two investigators who felt it push past.

In the week following the investigation I received a message from Kerri; she had met someone who had been connected with the building decades earlier and they had told her that a previous owner had been named Frank!

Marley's Winebar
1 Belgrave Cottage, Belgrave Road, Darwen, BB3 2RP
Telephone: 01254 706823

ECCLESTON
BYGONE TIMES

Having been associated for most of my life with the world of ghosts and hauntings, it is not surprising that those close to me are sometimes subjected to a visitation from the other side, and that is exactly what happened to my mother, Liz, some years ago.

Bygone Times.

We decided to take a trip to Bygone Times in Eccleston, a one-time mill now converted into three large warehouses show-casing everything from curios to collectables. This extremely popular nod to yesteryear is exactly the kind of afternoon trip an antique enthusiast, like my mother, enjoys.

After looking at the fine furniture and taking a stroll down the cobbled alleyway, which was unearthed during restoration in 1987, my mother had an encounter which she has talked about ever since. As she walked past a large piece of oak furniture, she felt a hand push her gently from the side. It was forceful and she assumed it was my father who was walking behind her at the time, but upon turning around to see what he wanted, she was surprised to find there was no one there. My mother went on to say that the prod was in no way threatening, quite friendly, in fact.

Who knows who this friendly phantasm is? Ghosts are often connected not to the building where they are encountered, but to the objects which inhabit the building. Could this ghost have been connected to one of the many fine and ancient antiques in the centre? With so many on offer there may well be other shades of the past lingering in the environs, waiting for a new home to be supplied by a keen buyer. It is not perhaps a surprise that with relics from each of the world wars, and artefacts from centuries long gone, times past and present collide here, at Bygone Times.

Bygone Times.
Grove Mill. The Green, Eccleston, Chorley. PR7 5PD
01257 451889
www.bygonetimes.co.uk

HESKIN HALL

T his ivy-clad Tudor mansion was built in 1548. It has passed through the hands of many famous Lancastrian families, including the Molyneux, the Kershaws and, most recently, the Lilfords, who occupied the building until 1969, when it became a training and educational establishment for Blackburn College.

Heskin Hall.

Today the building has undergone complete restoration and has been converted back, at least in appearance, to how it might have been when it was originally constructed. Oak-panelled rooms, baronial fireplaces, priest holes and studded oak doors are now the backdrop for the Hall's latest role – as a unique antique centre.

As with most old houses ghosts are thought to be lingering among the *objets d'art*. They are said to be those of a young Roman Catholic girl and an older man. During the Civil War the Hall was a resting place for Oliver Cromwell, as well as being a site for hanging religious martyrs. It is from this era that the stories originate.

The young girl is said to be the unfortunate victim of a priest who hung her as a public display of his conversion from Catholicism to Protestantism. Fate dealt the priest an equally grim hand though when soldiers, not convinced of his conversion, proceeded to hang him from the same spot! The last resident of Heskin Hall, Lady Lilford, is on record as describing the haste of some of her houseguests to depart following sightings of ghosts during their stay with her. I myself experienced a strange sensation when I visited the Hall. As I entered the front bedroom on the left of the house I felt I was not alone. It was as if unseen eyes were upon me, watching and observing. I have been back to the Hall many times since but never experienced that odd feeling again.

Heskin Hall
Wood Lane, Eccleston, Chorley, PR7 5PA
Telephone: 01257 452044

FOULRIDGE
THE NEW INN

It is said that this village gets its unusual name from a quote supposedly uttered from the mouth of Oliver Cromwell himself when he declared, 'This is a foul ridge on which to fight, we will meet the enemy on lower

The New Inn, Foulridge.

ground,' as his army prepared for battle on a moor nearby. The New Inn is tucked away on a back street in the village and is reputedly the most haunted pub in the Pendle district.

Barry Shepherd, the current landlord, settled at the pub in 1997. Not long after his arrival, a vase of dried flowers, which was located in the snug, was upturned and strewn across the floor each night for an entire week. On the seventh night his wife shouted at the ghost: 'Will you stop throwing these flowers around and annoying me!' It has never happened since.

Customers have reported seeing a ghostly male form descending the staircase from the landlord's quarters, walking across the snug, which is the most haunted area of the pub, and moving towards the back door. Poltergeist-like behaviour has also been witnessed, with sets of keys amongst other things being moved around by unseen hands.

Some years ago, a medium came here as a customer. She told Barry that the building was haunted by a 'mischievous friendly ghost'. Barry tends to agree. For instance, many female customers have complained that they feel 'watched', 'spooked' or 'uncomfortable' in the far cubicle of the ladies' toilets.

But mischievous is not a word you could use to describe an encounter witnessed by Barry after midnight one night in April 2005. He had locked up and was doing some routine cleaning when something caught his eye in the main bar. He looked up and saw a 7 ft tall, dark, solid figure coming out of the table 5 area. It floated across the floor and went into the ladies' where it disappeared from view. It made the hairs on the back of his neck stand up. Barry immediately turned on all the lights in the building and went into the toilets and, although there was nothing to be seen, it was like walking into a freezer. So he hurried out, switched off all the lights and ran upstairs to his flat, making sure he locked the door to the bar as he went. He couldn't sleep for over a week after seeing the phantom and hoped never to see it again.

The next month a cleaner at the pub was mopping the floor of the gents toilet. As she looked up, there was the solid black figure pressed up against the glass of the window staring in at her. It couldn't have been a customer as the inn was closed at the time and the area where the figure was standing was not accessible to the public. She was absolutely terrified and ran out of the room screaming.

So, who is the ghost haunting the New Inn? The local belief is that it is a Cavalier who was killed during the Civil War, but perhaps the fact that the building used to be a Quakers' Meeting House and a number of the Quakers themselves are buried beneath the dining room could explain some of the ghostly goings on?

When Veronica and I wandered around the inn, she reported that there was a mischievous young boy, aged around 14 in appearance, haunting the building. She could hear the name Johnny being called.

I asked Barry if this meant any sense to him and he told me that many of the old local drinkers called the ghost Tommy so perhaps Veronica had misheard 'Tommy' as 'Johnny'.

I took her into the dining room where she said there were several spirits, the most powerful being a lady who 'is very devoted to a religious belief'. She described her as short in stature, about 5 ft 3 ins, wearing a black dress, white undergarment and a white cap tied underneath her chin. This sounded like the garb of a Quaker and later I showed Veronica a picture of a Quaker woman, which, she said, matched that of the ghost she had seen.

Barry wanted to find out who the male figure was and asked Veronica to take a walk around the ladies' loo and table 5 area. After concentrating her feelings for a few moments she described a big man, strong and muscular, with a connection with horses. She saw him making horseshoes. She did not feel comfortable with this spirit, as he had a menacing character and clearly did not like women, and refused to communicate with the spirit further. Barry told us that this made a lot of sense to him because at one time the building was a blacksmith's and there had been a stable over the section where the ladies' toilet is now situated.

So, we were unable to find evidence of a ghostly Cavalier, but did uncover a mischievous child spirit, a gentle Quaker lady and a menacing blacksmith.

The New Inn
Skipton Old Road, Foulridge, Colne, BB8 7PD
Telephone: 01282 864068

HAIGH, WIGAN
HAIGH HALL

Noted as Wigan's most prominent and enduring landmark, Haigh Hall, which dates back to 1850 and built on the site of an earlier hall, was the former ancestral home of the Earl of Crawford and Balcarres. It enjoys the mystery of a chequered and fragmented history, with much of its past unrecorded. Therefore, rumours and whispered tales have now filled in the gaps creating a rich tapestry of folk tales and ghost stories.

Perhaps the most celebrated legend dates from 1295 when Sir William Bradshaigh married Mabel Norris de Haigh. A popular version of this tragic story dictates that soon after betrothal William was summoned to fight in the Holy Wars and was absent for so long that he was assumed dead. Apparently widowed, Lady Mabel found solace in the arms of a Welsh lord and soon married for a second time. In 1302 Sir William returned to Lancashire disguised as a palmer (a pilgrim from the Holy Land) and observed activities at the Hall from a safe distance. Lady Mabel, glimpsing the palmer, observed his close likeness to her first husband and became deeply upset. Whereupon, Sir William, seeing his former love in such distress, made himself known. The Welsh knight fled Haigh but was pursued and overtaken by Sir William who killed him near Newton-le-Willows at a spot now known as 'The Bloody Stone'. The stone has long since been removed but was said to turn red as blood when rain fell upon it.

Sir William was outlawed for a year and a day for the murder of the Welsh lord and Lady Mabel was ordered to do penance by walking sackclothed and barefoot from Haigh Hall to the stone cross in Wigan Lane, which subsequently became known as Mab's Cross. She died in 1348 and was buried in the family vault with her husband at Wigan parish church. On the death of Mabel, Haigh Hall passed to a nephew of Sir William's and her restless ghost has been said to haunt the Hall and grounds ever since. A room in the house has been named Mab's Gallery because of her continued manifestations there, and the lane upon which she walked in penance is also said to be haunted by her restless shade, eternally paying for an innocent crime of love.

Veronica and I decided to visit the Hall to see whether she could shed more light on this tragic tale or perhaps uncover some new hauntings. As we approached the impressive exterior, she hesitated and asked if we could take a walk around the outside before entering the building. As we were ahead of schedule and it was a bright, sunny summer afternoon, I readily agreed, hoping that she was already picking up something of interest.

'I can see nurses and war uniforms,' she began. 'This house has been used for rehabilitation; a kind of hospital during a war. There is also a separate sad spirit that associates itself with the grounds more than the building – a lonely woman.' Could this be the wandering spirit of Mabel, I wondered, as we continued to walk around the grand mansion. 'There is a golden carriage pulled by horses clattering by,' Veronica said, as she stopped and strained her eyes as if to 'see' further into her vision. 'A man who liked to get his own way,' she continued. We were now at the entrance and I knocked on the door to be greeted by Ian who was to act as our guide around the Hall.

Our first stop was to be the magnificent ballroom where Ian told us that a painter had suffered a severe fright. He had been left in there overnight to try and get the work back on schedule after a delay, but in the morning he was terrified, reporting that he had heard a party going on in the next room – even though he was alone in the Hall at the time. Not surprisingly he declined to return. We were then told that there was a room on the second floor where guard dogs refuse to tread and which is now unused. Perhaps this was Mab's Gallery?

I asked Ian if the Hall had ever been used as a hospital and he said that it had during the last war. I then enquired whether a golden carriage and horses delivering a man who liked his own way made any sense to him and he replied that it could refer to the king who had visited there.

We made our way through the West Library, where the shadows of ladies in 'swirling crinoline dresses' caught Veronica's attention, before arriving at the door to the cellars. 'This house has lost its heart,' said Veronica. 'It is as if the spirit of the house has been ripped out – an heir failed to materialise.' Ian confirmed that was correct and that the last tenant sold the building to Wigan Council in 1945 because there was no heir to take it on.

We descended the slippery steps into a dank and never-ending labyrinth of tunnels and rooms. Ian told us that there had been no reported sightings here but Veronica located two different male entities. One was a gentleman with a flat cap whom she believed had been connected with the railways and had lived in a cottage in the grounds of the Hall. He had been occasionally employed to do odd jobs around the mansion and had been rewarded with little pay but plentiful ale from the supplies in the cellar. The other wraith was a man sporting a handlebar moustache and wearing a brown suit of the Victorian era. He refused to communicate with Veronica but she said his presence was considerably strong.

So, our visit to Haigh Hall proved fruitful. As well as the spectre of Lady Mabel, it seems that the Hall is home to the spirits of many others who have passed through its doors down the years.

Haigh Hall
Haigh Country Park, Haigh, Wigan, WN2 1PE
Telephone: 01942 832895
www.haighhall.net

HURST GREEN
THE PUNCH BOWL INN

This attractive country pub, dating back to 1793, is steeped in history. Once a row of cottages and, subsequently, a coaching inn, the building has rustic charm and promises a warm welcome. Notoriously linked with the infamous highwayman Ned King, the building is home to another ghost, as Veronica and I discovered when we visited recently.

Popular local legend dictates that a former landlord teamed up with Ned in an ingenious and highly criminal scheme to relieve visiting gentlemen and ladies of their valuables and grow rich themselves on the proceeds. Upon their arrival, the landlord would send word to Ned if guests were carrying loot worth lifting and, after partaking of the excellent fare and changing horses, they would be met by Ned just down the road. Here he would demand that they hand over their valuables or lose their life. This devilish partnership continued unabated for several years until eventually the authorities got wind of it and set about putting an end to Ned's nefarious career. They finally captured him in the barn next to the inn, now the dining room, and promptly put him to death by hanging on nearby Gallows Lane. His ghost is the most prevalent at the inn and it has been seen many times in the Minstrels' Gallery by those enjoying dinner below. Indeed, when I walked around the pub with Veronica, she continually looked up towards the gallery and later told me that she felt she was being watched.

Susan Burke, the land-lady, showed us around the various rooms of the inn but we had begun our investigation on the road outside. Veronica felt a male presence here. He was wearing a dark frock coat, high boots and a hat, and was carrying a riding crop. He also had a large scar down the side of his face. 'Deception, lies and death are associated with this spirit,' said Veronica.

Susan verified that the spectre of the highwayman is reputed to haunt the entire area, not just the Minstrels' Gallery inside. Indeed she has even

The Punch Bowl Inn.

witnessed the psychic echo of his horse galloping down the road at 1 o'clock in the morning. Her husband has encountered another spectral sound, this time that of a coach and horses, rattling past in broad daylight with nothing to account for what he clearly heard. They have experienced other phenomena as well, which she thought might be the work of a different spectre. Knives and forks jangling together in the kitchen have been reported by catering staff, mostly around the time of the full moon when paranormal activity is generally most rife.

Although Veronica failed to locate any spectral presence in the kitchen, she did encounter two further spirits in the upstairs bedrooms. The first was that of a young girl between the age of 14 and 16 who had been assaulted and had 'got her own back'. Veronica said she moved between rooms 4 and 5 and was particularly focussed on the window in room 5 where she was looking out into the garden.

The third ghost Veronica located was that of a gentleman scribe in room 4. The man, who was dressed in a black robe, showed Veronica a book and a wooden casket. This had once contained documents that could prove his rights, which had been stripped away from him. He was a very angry soul. After stating the name Thomas Elford, his spirit faded away, his message passed on.

We left the inn with images of Ned King, the young girl and the gentleman scribe planted firmly in our minds, and wondered what further activity Susan and her husband might encounter as they continue to live in this haunted hostelry.

The Punch Bowl Inn
Hurst Green, Clitheroe, BB7 9QW
Telephone: 01254 826209

LITTLE SINGLETON
MAINS HALL

I came across Mains Hall at Little Singleton quite by chance. When I began my research for this book, I immersed myself in local history archives, libraries and the internet, and it was here, through the technology of the 21st century, that I found the key to an ancient manor; an untapped treasure which I have visited several times since.

There has been a dwelling place of some kind on this site as far back as the Norman Conquest in 1066 and possibly even earlier. Due to its prime location on the banks of the River Wyre, a house built here would have enjoyed great benefits, being close to the main shipping areas of Lancashire, Skippool, Fleetwood and Lancaster. According to historic sources, the manor of Singleton was split during the medieval period resulting in Great Singleton – containing the chapel and village now referred to as Singleton village – and Little Singleton, where Mains Hall stands.

The current Hall is a Grade II listed, 16th-century manor house and, as you might expect, is steeped in local legend. It is believed that some of the beams contained within the house are part of a much earlier building dating back to medieval times. Local archive material refers to a knight, Sir Alan de Singleton, being given the land by King John and residing here as Lord of the Manor in the early 13th century. Sir Alan was connected to Sir Adam de Singleton who built

Mains Hall.

Chingle Hall, on the outskirts of Goosnargh, another haunted Lancastrian manor house. Later in the 14th century, a second knight, Sir Adam Banastre (Banister), was incumbent at Mains Hall. There are suggestions that the original old building might have had links to Cockersand Abbey, as ancient maps refer to it as Monks Hall. Possibly, these monks were tenant farmers of the local lord of the time. Certainly, tales of phantom monks have been blamed on the alleged burial of twelve lay brothers, thought to be victims of the plague, beneath ancient trees in the grounds.

Following the Dissolution of the Monasteries, the estate became the property of the Earl of Derby in 1536. It then passed to Alice, Countess of Derby, who subsequently sold it to William Hesketh, owner of Rufford Old Hall. Scant records exist for the later Tudor and Elizabethan eras but it is recorded that several generations of the Hesketh family lived at the Hall in the time of James I and Charles I, and carried out much needed restoration on the estate. Thomas Hesketh, along with his second wife Mary, restored the old chapel and barns in 1686, leaving their mark in the brickwork, which can still be seen today. A local historian, when writing about his visit in 1853, speaks of the original Tudor banqueting hall thus: '... on the west, the wing now destroyed, a very antique building, within which was a hall-part, having a huge open chimney, and wainscoted with fluted oak of the reign of Henry VIII, now rotting unheeded in the garrets of the hall.'

The original Hall has also been home to many other famous local families, including the Fitzherbert-Brockholes, the most well known of which was Maria Fitzherbert, mistress and later 'wife' to George IV. The Prince Regent – later to become King George IV – torn between love and duty, illicitly courted the young Maria, far away from the gossip and speculation of London society. It has been suggested by some historical sources that the Prince visited her here at the Mains estate. The lengthy courtship was followed by a secret marriage, which lasted nine years. However, the union was dissolved by an Act of Parliament in 1795, releasing the Prince so that he could wed Princess Caroline of Brunswick; apparently a 'better' match as no prince could inherit the throne if married to a Catholic. It is rumoured that the first wedding took place in the chapel at Mains Hall, sadly long gone from the estate.

From the early 1990s, under the ownership of Roger and Adele Yeomans, the building was used as a bed and breakfast establishment and later upgraded to a luxury country house hotel. During this time, scores of guests reported nightly visitations from the beyond. The house is now used as the Yeomans' private residence and is closed to the public. An extensive long-term restoration project has been instigated, which will transform the Hall back to its former glory.

In 2004 a replica Tudor banqueting hall was built in the grounds on the site of the former original Great Hall. It now hosts lavish weddings, allowing those with a sense of history to bask in the rich heritage on their special day. Roger and Adele were the first to wed here and now hundreds have followed in their footsteps. With the various additions and architectural alterations, priest holes, and a 'stone circle', plus the construction of the replica Great Hall in the grounds, it is not surprising that a variety of colourful ghost stories have become attached to the place over the years.

I thought it would be interesting to see if Veronica could grasp any sense of the past in the replica Tudor banqueting hall, and so that was where our investigation began one May afternoon. As soon as we crossed the threshold she made straight for the enormous fireplace at the far end of the Hall. 'There is a man here, 50 to 60 years old, with lots of facial hair and he is in a desperate hurry. He is wearing a small skullcap and throwing a heavy grey woollen cloak over his shoulder. He is preparing to leave this place.' She carried on, 'There are horses outside, I can hear them. He is collecting his belongings: a book, a crucifix and various other trappings of priesthood. He is clearly in fear of his life – my heart is thumping very fast as I am experiencing his dread.' As Adele and I watched, Veronica's arms became covered in large goose bumps, despite it being a very warm afternoon.

The Great Hall (left) with Mains Hall next to it.

Adele told us that Veronica had picked up on the spirit of Cardinal William Allen, a one-time Catholic priest who died in 1594 aged 62 and had used the former Great Hall as a hiding place during the times of Catholic intolerance. He was connected with the estate after his sister had married into the Hesketh family. When the old building was pulled down a secret priest hide was discovered behind the fireplace and a cup, crucifix and some documents were also found. This all seemed to tally with what Veronica had felt and so we made our way across the garden towards Mains Hall itself.

The driveway and buildings nearby once formed a courtyard where horses would have been stabled – another correct 'feeling' which Veronica had mentioned. As we walked in the bright sunshine I asked Adele about the phantom monks. She mentioned a newspaper article that had been published in 1950. In it the Hall's owner at the time not only talks of the plague-stricken monks but also records a ghostly coach trundling up to the house on dark nights when the air is still.

A man who lived there in the 1960s contacted Adele and told her that one night he and several friends saw the horse-drawn carriage approaching the stables. The earliest written record of supernatural phenomena at the Hall dates from a book printed in the 1920s, which stated that Mains Hall was deserted as it was believed to be haunted and 'no locals will go near it'. There are also said to be two ley lines that cross the property and converge in the gardens – one runs beneath the Great Hall and the other beneath Mains Hall itself – they are said to 'conduct paranormal energies'.

Veronica had been quiet as we had approached the Hall, but now she was in full communication with the other side. We paused at the unremarkable façade for her to 'link' with the place. She said there were many spirits there, from various time periods in history. Some were memories of the past and oblivious to the living, others knew that we were there and had been waiting for us. One in particular was very prominent – a woman who had a child with her. Adele unlocked the front door and we stepped into the Jacobean entrance hall, which is decorated with ancient wooden panelling taken from the Earl of Saville's estate. Veronica walked across the hallway to the bottom of the main staircase, where she stopped and stared towards the top. 'She is here now,' she said quietly, looking directly at Adele. 'She is telling me she has shown herself to you.' Adele replied that she had seen her standing there many times. Feeling left out I walked to the top of the staircase where Adele warned me to be careful as other people had felt the spectre rush past and force them out of the way. We ascended and went into the Tudor Room, which Adele informed me was the most haunted area of the house. Veronica was busy placing her hands on the walls, trying to make a connection with the past.

'I can see her clearly in this room; she is looking out of a window which I cannot see, as if she is waiting for someone. She wears a blue velvet gown, plainly embroidered, a choker with a red jewel and has brown hair. There is a great sadness within her. She is crying desperately, a sense of loss, a child has been lost at a tender age. Despite the name of the room she is not a Tudor ghost, from her appearance I would judge it to be Victorian and she is a young spirit, not having yet reached her 30th birthday. She will show herself only to women; she has a deep mistrust of men.'

Adele had been nodding throughout, and said that she had named the unhappy young woman 'Lily' and spoke to her all the time. 'She hears you,' replied Veronica. 'She cannot rest and you are her solace. There is a strong connection between you both, which is very rare and special. She is moving now, gliding towards you across the room.' Moments later tears were streaming down Adele's face. I asked her if she was all right. 'She has just touched my hair,' she replied.

It was obvious to Veronica and me that a deep psychological link existed between Adele and Lily, which transcended time and logic and which I have occasionally come across before with people who share their homes with the dead. After a moment I asked Adele if she knew who Lily was. She told me that she had been in contact with a lady who had lived at the Hall as a child. The lady's mother had been employed as a servant, was called Lily (Lilian) and had dearly loved working in the house, often wishing she would return one day. Sadly she passed away before her wish was granted. It is here that the story becomes confusing as it is Lily's employer, not Lily herself, that matches the visual description given by Veronica and has been seen by Adele on many occasions. This lady (whose identity I have been asked to conceal) endured a sad existence at Mains Hall, losing a child by miscarriage and being trapped in a loveless marriage. She was 'entombed' at Mains Hall and often sought solace in talking with Lily as she cried on the staircase or in the Tudor Room, waiting for her unfaithful husband to return.

So it seems that the visual ghost (the employer) and Lily (the servant) have become intertwined; the various elements of information, however, are all correct. Since my visit, a team of ghost hunters investigating the house reported hearing a baby crying in this area of the Hall and one experienced the curious sensation of 'something very small creeping past her ankles'. Using a ouija board, they contacted a woman who told them that the sound they had heard was the spirit of a baby with the initials 'JH'. Could this be the baby that Adele has seen in ghostly form, drenched in blood and crawling across the floor in the room? Adele's daughter Beccy has also heard the sombre sound of sobbing echoing around the room; perhaps that of a weeping mother? Even 'down to earth' workmen have experienced the unmistakable feeling of having their hair stroked whilst working in the area. Adele believes that Lily predominantly haunts the Tudor Room, the main staircase, the former priest hide (where she looks out of a window long bricked up) and the master bedroom, where Adele and Roger now sleep. One night during the full moon Adele witnessed the apparition float around the bed and watch over Roger as he slept, oblivious to her presence.

Whilst Adele had been telling me Lily's tale, Veronica had retraced her steps and was standing on the steps that lead up to the Tudor Room from the main stairwell. She was obviously agitated by something. She went on to describe seeing another spectre, a small slender man wearing a black robe who was from another era. He was a kindly gentleman, a holy man or priest. Veronica then became overwhelmed by a feeling of being stifled and of wanting to desperately escape from the place. Adele went on to explain that the area where Veronica was standing used to be a priest hide behind a former fireplace where it is thought Catholic priests would have hid whilst Protestant forces were searching the house for those disobeying the faith laws during the times of religious persecution. I asked Veronica if this was the same priest, Cardinal Allen, that we had encountered in the Great Hall but she replied that it was a different man. His attire was different and she felt that he had died there in agony. It was common practice for priest hides to be incorporated into chimneys and, in order to 'flush out the priests', soldiers would demand that all fires be lit and kept alight for several days. Thereby, the priests would either give themselves up or, unable to breathe for the thick smoke, would suffer a grim end by slowly burning to death.

I decided it was time to give Veronica some respite from the choking sensation and asked her to move across the chamber towards the Upper Hall. As we walked beneath the overhanging gallery she stopped. 'There is another here,' she said. It seemed a third spirit was vying for her attention before we left the Tudor Room and Adele and I waited patiently as she closed her eyes to make the vision in her mind clearer. 'This is another man,' she said. 'He is a nasty piece of work – cruel, dominant, demanding. I get the name "James". He is big built and wearing a long frock coat. He would have been unfair with his staff when he was Lord of the Manor here, and I feel he would pick on the weak, rejoicing in their fear.'

Adele told us that she believed this was a man who had been strung up and hung from the very beam we were standing beneath, and that on one occasion this unseen 'corpse' had kicked her housekeeper in the stomach as it swayed back and forth. On another occasion, whilst cleaning the room, her vacuum cleaner had been tampered with – inexplicably turning itself on and off.

Leaving the most haunted room behind we made our way into the Upper Hall, Here Adele told us that there has been a sighting of a young man wearing a brown bomber jacket and jeans. Veronica could pick up on no particular story, suggesting that he was 'merely a psychic imprint on the atmosphere'. Next we climbed another set of stairs and entered room 10, which was undergoing restoration at the time and was devoid of any furnishings. Adele told us that when the building was a hotel this was a family room and every time the maids came in it was filled with large black flies. No one could understand where these came from as the windows were always closed and often it was mid winter – not the season for flies. Veronica, though, linked with the mild spirit of an austere, yet friendly, lady. 'She is sitting on a rocking chair singing a lullaby to a tiny child,' she began, and went on to describe a wooden crib and a rocking horse, and a cast-iron fireplace in the wall. Adele said that several people had heard children's nursery rhymes being sung in various areas of the building.

I scanned the room but, as usual, I saw nothing: no fireplace, no crib and no ghost. Adele told Veronica that she was linking with the room below, which used to be the nursery. Veronica paused, communicating on a psychic wavelength with her spirit guide. 'This was the nanny's or governess's bedroom; her presence is very strong here. I am hearing a voice saying "I'm Nanny".' Then Veronica continued, 'There is a young boy appearing now, he has long fair hair; his appearance reminds me of Thomas Gainsborough's painting The Blue Boy. He is telling me to go downstairs.' With that clear instruction from the ghost child I asked Adele if she would take us down to the former nursery on the ground floor. As we descended, Adele related the occasion when a local radio presenter had been recording in the room. The presenter had jumped out of her skin as she felt the floorboards beneath her feet 'bashed' hard from the room below, a room which was locked and deserted. At the same time a professional cameraman had been unable to take any photographs of the room; his equipment malfunctioned yet worked fine in other areas of the Hall.

Returning to the Upper Hall on our way downstairs, Adele stopped to tell us that two visitors had reported seeing 'pin point lights' here one night, which are often thought to be the beginning of a ghostly manifestation. The same visitors, who had an interest in the hauntings, had conducted a séance in which they claim to have contacted the spirits of two children, Edward and Jessica, who they believed had been responsible for the ghost lights. The child identifying itself as Jessica also communicated that she 'watched the housekeeper' (who was present during the séance) and that she liked the way the housekeeper said hello to her. This revelation shocked the sitters when the housekeeper revealed that she always greets the ghosts when she enters the Hall to carry out her chores. She also reported that she had felt many times that a young girl was trying to hold her hand when walking along the downstairs corridor in the house.

Before we went back downstairs we stopped off in the Master Bedroom where Adele has seen Lily in solid apparition form. Here Veronica heard a clanking of metal as if someone in armour was walking around. She described the figure as strong and powerful, and commented that people must have heard his footsteps before as they were so loud. Adele agreed that many had, adding that this might be the ghost of the knight Sir Alan de Singleton who is thought to have built the original house. Other phenomena reported here include the indentation of a body appearing in freshly-made beds; the movement of objects, including keys, shoes and a hairbrush; whispering in sleepers' ears and a loud rattling of the door latch. One incident of note occurred whilst the room was a hotel bedroom. On this occasion, a visitor had rung down to reception to request towels, which had subsequently been delivered and placed on the bed by Adele. A short while later the same visitor, somewhat angry, phoned once again saying they had not received the towels they had asked for. When the room was searched these were found stuffed in the bottom of the shower tray. At other times children have been heard playing and laughing in this room – some people have even felt something invisible sit on the end of the bed or even climb in with them! Could this be Edward and Jessica who have been reported in other areas of the Hall?

We went back downstairs and made our way to room 9 – the one-time nursery. En route we found ourselves walking a long windowless corridor. Here the spirits of unseen children are said to 'brush the hands of the living as if encouraging them along to the nursery' and a strange anomalous photograph showing a 'blue streak of energy' was caught in recent months. We passed another priest hide and a medieval door, which had been unearthed in the grounds, before arriving at the threshold of room 9.

Upon entering I was not surprised to see that it did not resemble a nursery at all. When the Hall was in use as a hotel this was a luxury suite and still houses the grand canopied bed and adjoining bathroom. 'That's where the cast-iron fireplace was,' said Adele as she pointed to a wall, two storeys below the location where Veronica had 'seen' it whilst in the governess's quarters in the gables far above us. 'I have been told by a previous owner that a young male child died in this room from a hole in the heart,' she added. Having followed the instructions of the ghostly boy in blue, we awaited Veronica's impressions of the chamber. 'He has faded away because a man has come into the room,' she said. 'He is saying nothing; it is as if he does not want me to know anything about him.' After a few moments I asked Adele to put us out of our misery and elaborate on this ghostly male. She related that several years earlier a female hotel guest had stayed the night in the room and reported that she had enjoyed a sexual encounter with an invisible suitor in the dead of night! Far from being frightened by the experience she retired to her room early the next night, hoping that her spectral suitor would make a return visit; which apparently, after she had heard a shuffling outside the door, he did. This strange phenomenon, although hard to believe, actually has a long-standing pedigree in the annals of psychic research where it is known as an incubus. Another house guest, this time a friend of Adele's daughter, found it hard to sleep in the room when he stayed one evening. He reported incessant footsteps from the room above him, discovering in the morning that the room in question had been vacant all night.

Leaving the ghostly boy and the incubus behind we went into room 8 next door. Veronica began laughing almost as soon as we had entered the bedroom. 'There is a character here, a small lady with round glasses and a white apron – she is carrying a rolling pin and darting about,' she said. 'I have never heard of her before,' replied Adele, 'although we do have strange things happen in this room.' Veronica had the impression that the lady was a former cook who was lingering around in a state of confusion. 'She likes playing tricks,' she concluded. Adele understood now, as on many occasions whilst the Hall was a hotel and even since it has been closed to the general public, people have been locked into the room from the outside. On one occasion a workman and Adele were locked in and on another a loud knocking was heard on the door – even though no one was seen. So why would a cook be haunting this area of the house and playing ghostly japes on the living? Adele speculated that the room may once have been part of the kitchen as during the 19th century the entire layout of the building was rearranged. This might also explain why the spirit appeared to be 'darting about' in a state of confusion' – maybe she cannot find the old kitchen!

Our next stop was the dining room, which enjoys wonderful views of the River Wyre at the back of the Hall. Here Veronica found an 'elegant lady pacing up and down' who 'fancies herself as royalty; but is clearly not'. As Veronica explained what she was seeing, she curtseyed as if meeting someone important.

'Why did you curtsey?' I asked. Unaware of her own action she looked puzzled, and it was then that Adele filled in the next piece of this psychic jigsaw puzzle. 'You are sensing Maria Fitzherbert.' Veronica and I looked blankly at Adele, not immediately recognising the name. 'She lived in this house in the 18th century and secretly married the Prince Regent, later King George IV. She was a renowned beauty and popular socialite. Although the union was dissolved to allow the Prince to marry a Protestant princess, records show that this was a disaster, and he later returned to his beloved Maria at Mains Hall. Sadly his position never allowed him to commit fully to her and she died never having married again.' 'That explains her reason for lingering here,' decided Veronica, 'she was ill-treated, dismissed and died broken-hearted.'

We walked underneath the archway that separates the dining area from the winter snug; this was formerly the bar when the house was in use as a hotel. Adele told us that a group of beekeepers had been staying several years ago and were making merry in the bar one night when they saw a misty figure wearing 'the garb of a Cavalier'. This sighting could make historical sense as a battle took place nearby in 1715 during the Jacobite Rebellion. History tells us that local marauders sought food and shelter here from the lady of the house. Other reports of Cavaliers in the house tell of a ghostly swordfight that was re-enacted in spectral form on the main staircase, resulting in one unfortunate succumbing to the other's blade. In the previous year there had been another incident in the snug, which was blamed on the same Cavalier ghost; on this occasion a visitor felt the back of her coat tugged downwards with great force. When she turned around there was no one to be seen. The room has been recently refurbished, rewired and redecorated but still odd things occur, including clocks which stop working for no apparent reason.

Leaving the not-so-snug snug, Adele whisked us off to the next area where unusual activity had been reported – the library. Concealed behind the fireplace amid ancient book-filled shelves lies another priest hole; a false bookshelf moves aside when depressed allowing the inquisitive to enter this hidden and haunted refuge.

Does the spirit of Cardinal Allen haunt this area of the house? His ghost has been glimpsed crossing the Jacobean entrance hall and entering this room on several occasions. An even stranger phenomenon occurs here, one that is not easy to explain. It involves the anomalous function of an antique clock that adorns the mantelpiece. At times this 'shell' comes to life and has been heard chiming; incredible since the piece contains no workings and has no way of chiming, or indeed of creating the 'tick tock' that has also been observed in this room where no operational timepiece resides.

Before we concluded our investigation we were invited into Roger's study, a room which is not usually thought of as being haunted. Veronica was clearly tired from her psychic exertions and numerous encounters with the spectres of Mains Hall and I did not expect her to pick up on anything else, but surprisingly she did manage to contact a final wraith; this time one who had been personally known to both Adele and Roger. 'He is a portly man wearing a patterned waistcoat and sporting a monocle; he reminds me of Charles Dickens' 'Pickwick' character,' she said to Roger, who was keen to see what would be discovered in his den. I noticed Adele and Roger glance at each other as if they understood the comment, yet they remained silent – eager to hear what else Veronica would pick up. 'He is making me laugh, quite a joker, I like him – he is showing me a large brandy as if this is his home and he is welcoming me in.' By now Roger was nodding and smiling, 'I know who that is!' he said. I asked him to elaborate further. 'He was a live-in resident whilst the Hall was a hotel. He spent his last two years here instead of going into a retirement home and he certainly liked a brandy,' he answered. 'He was a real old-fashioned "country gent" and had a great sense of fun. I remember him having a remote controlled duck with which he used to entertain the children on the pond in the grounds and he died peacefully in his room here. You have hit the nail on the head though, as he always wore a waistcoat and monocle.'

After a long afternoon exploring every nook and cranny of the ancient house and grounds, Veronica and I said our farewells and made our way home, arranging to return for further investigations soon. In my reckoning that makes 27 ghosts haunting Mains Hall; clearly putting it at the top of Lancashire's haunted hotspots. I have since stumbled across a BBC website on which a previous resident of the Hall has stated: 'If there is ever an option of being a ghost after death and choosing a place to haunt, then I will return, as it was the only place I was ever happy.' Perhaps some day that will make it 28 ghosts, happily wandering around 'Lancashire's Most Haunted House'.

Mains Hall
Mains Lane, Little Singleton, FY6 7LE
Telephone: 01253 885130
www.mainshall.co.uk

LITTLEBOROUGH
STUBLEY HALL

At the invitation of Lord and Lady Speakman, one night of the full moon in December 2001, I took a team of psychic investigators from the Ghost Research Foundation to Stubley Hall at Littleborough. Originally constructed as a home for Ralph de Stobbeley in the 13th century, it was rebuilt in the 16th century and, in more recent years was a successful pub and restaurant. Not long ago it was purchased by the Speakmans who have a lengthy restoration plan underway and they called us in to elaborate on the hauntings said to be associated with this magnificent house.

Tales of a ghostly woman have been connected to the Hall for many years. She is thought to be a young bride called Fatima who was engaged to Ralph de Stobbeley himself. But her tale is not one of happiness. After her beloved left her to fight in the Crusades, he was tempted by another and set in line a turn of events that was to reverberate through the centuries at the old manor. Grief stricken by the news Fatima fell into a deep despair and died a lost and unhappy young woman. Months later, when Ralph returned to his country home, it is said that she was glimpsed watching from the woods that surrounded the Hall. A painting commemorating this sad event now hangs over one of the grand fireplaces – a permanent reminder of the house's troubled past.

Helen Garner, who used to manage Stubley Hall when it was a restaurant, is on record as saying: 'I drove up to the Hall early one morning and noticed a light in one of the windows. After unlocking the door I found a lighted candle on the windowsill near the main hall. It had clearly only been burning for a matter of minutes as the wax was still warm. I know it wasn't there the night before when I locked up, as I was the only key holder at the time.'

Could Fatima still be waiting for her betrothed to meet her in the afterlife? It has been suggested that this candle was left by her as a guiding light to bring Ralph back to the place where she believed she had found eternal love. Many think that her presence still haunts the hallways of the old Hall, watching and waiting hopelessly for the return of one who is long dead. She makes her presence known mostly to young ladies – and, in particular, young brides – who visit the building, by tripping them up, ruffling their hair and tugging on veils and jewellery. As a fitting end to the tale of Fatima and Ralph, it is said that he dropped dead years later, having heard the melancholy notes of harp music echoing from the surrounding woods – a musical summoning to the beyond perhaps, for in life Fatima was an accomplished harpist.

The ghost of Ralph de Stobbeley 'overshadows' medium Angela Borrows (being supported with hands in the air).

Although we did not encounter the ghost of Fatima during our investigation, we did experience one of the building's other spectral residents – that of Ralph de Stobbeley himself, who appears in his former bedroom. As we were setting up our ghost hunting equipment, which monitors the environment for unnatural atmospheres and temperatures, we were called into a small room near the current front door. Angela Borrows, one of the mediums taking part in the research, was standing in the middle of the room describing the feeling of an intense pressure forcing her backwards and down towards the floor. Two investigators caught her as she was about to fall and could also feel the force pushing down with great strength. Another medium, Diana Jarvis, was next to encounter the spirit as it moved across the room to focus on her, again pushing her backwards with strong intensity. The rest of the group watched entranced as she gradually appeared to lean backwards at such an angle that she should have fallen to the ground, yet she was supported in mid air by no apparent means! Diana later described the experience from her perspective, telling us that she felt the arms of a strong man around her waist and was supported against his muscular chest. Could this have been the ghost of Ralph de Stobbeley, up to his old tricks even after death?

Following the experience with Ralph, which is now remembered by the group as 'like a scene from the *Exorcist* film', we concluded that the spirit of the former Lord of the Manor is still very much in residence at his old home. Research has also identified two further ghosts: a Roundhead soldier, who has been seen leaning against a fireplace staring moodily into the flames, and a little girl child who has been sighted skipping happily in the fields surrounding this fascinating house.

As we dismantled our equipment, I was surprised to find that one of the leads connecting a camera to some recording apparatus had been physically undone by some unseen hand – this required a great deal of force. Perhaps the ghost of Ralph de Stobbeley does not want his escapades caught on film!

MIDDLETON
TONGE HALL

Tonge Hall is a typical haunted house, with an overgrown garden, broken windows and a roof set to cave in. Owned by Mr Norman Wolstencroft and his wife Rosemary, who divide their time between the Hall and another home in Scotland, the Tudor mansion dates back to the 16th century and is allegedly the home of four sprightly spectres.

I visited, with a team of investigators, as the sun was setting, casting long shadows over the crumbling black and white house, and was given a warm welcome by Norman who showed us around his unusual home, mostly derelict and in need of serious repair. I had decided to undertake some research at the Hall after a group of American ghost hunters had achieved some good results when investigating with medium Linda McKenzie, who was forcibly pushed by an unseen force here.

We decided to concentrate our activities on the exterior while there was still some light and so, armed with an infra red video camera and some other equipment, we began monitoring the grounds for signs of anything out of the ordinary. These kinds of experiments are a matter of course on any ghost hunt and they usually yield little or no results. We were therefore extremely excited when we thought we had captured something strange on camera. We quickly rewound the tape and played the recording back on a large screen for everyone to see. Sure enough there, on the film, was recorded an anomalous image of what looks like dense mist, which shifted and contorted before moving out of site around a corner of the house. Following this rare success we wondered what else the evening ahead might have in store for us at Tonge Hall.

After retreating from the gardens back into the candlelit mansion, Norman told us of one of the spirits that is said to haunt the house – a young girl whose pitiful crying echoes from the cavernous cellars that stretch beneath the building. We decided to investigate, making a map of the layout of the house as we went. After waiting for some time in the dank cellar for any sign of the child spirit, we were summoned back to the main house by the senior investigator, Wendy Simpson, who had made an intriguing discovery in the hallway. 'Look what has appeared,' she said, pointing to four upturned drinks coasters which had been placed in a vaguely square alignment on the floor of an otherwise completely empty room. 'They were not here before,' she added. I asked each member of the team independently if they had seen the coasters on the floor earlier and each was emphatic that they had definitely not been there. Why they had been deposited there is a mystery, as are so many features of experiences in haunted houses.

Throughout the night, feelings of being watched, cold spots and an 'arc of light' were recorded in our logbooks but the spirits had not yet finished toying with the living, as we found out during a ouija board experiment held in the Great Hall in the early hours. An entity calling itself William communicated with the team and although we could not place the name within the history of the house, Norman told us that William was the name of his uncle who had died after being shot in the knee …

MORECAMBE
BARCLAYS BANK

In my files I have an account from a Maureen Claxton of Morecambe who used to work as a night-time cleaner at Barclays Bank in the town. The bank is housed in a very old building, which, she suggests, may have a turbulent past.

'It was always uncomfortable in that building,' Maureen explained. 'I used to work alone, although I always felt as if there was someone else with me, watching from the shadows.' As a psychically sensitive person, Maureen has encountered many different forms of ghostly activity in her lifetime, including seeing the ghosts of five Canadian airmen in a house where they used to lodge in years past, but even that experience was nothing compared to the fear she felt at Barclays.

She said that the cleaning equipment was kept down a winding staircase in the cellar, and she hated going down there. On one occasion she remembered the vacuum cleaner switching itself off and the lights going out of their own accord. There was an ungodly smell in there as well – it seemed to come and go without any breeze inside the building. In the end she felt so uncomfortable that she left the job. Maureen later worked as a cleaner in Ladbrokes, which is situated next door to Barclays, and she believes the ghost followed her there. On her first day the new vacuum blew up when she touched it and she was convinced it was the ghost from next door.

So, who is haunting the branch of Barclays in Morecambe? Is it a spirit connected to the building, or perhaps one connected to Maureen? Maybe this tale lends weight to the theory that wandering ghosts are attracted to people with the ability to sense them and that, whether in a haunted building or not, those who are receptive will always attract those on the other side.

NELSON
THE BAPTIST CHURCH

My informant, Joe Spencer, told me of a strange encounter with a mysterious woman that he experienced whilst undertaking renovation work on the Baptist church in Nelson. Being a down-to-earth kind of man, Joe – and his brother who was working with him at the time – could not be described as 'prone to the imaginary' as some people might be, and I found him to be a credible witness.

'My brother was hard at work in one room of the building,' Joe told me, 'and I was next door making a cup of tea for us both. As I turned to switch on the kettle a woman strutted into the room, went to the sink to wash her hands, and then promptly left again without even glancing in my direction or bidding me a good morning! Moments after she had left I went in to see my brother and asked who she was. He looked at me confused and told me that he had no idea who I was talking about. The weird thing is, the layout of the building is such that she must have gone past him both to enter the kitchen and to leave, yet my brother had seen no one. An immediate search also showed that the church was deserted and there was no explanation for who she was, or why she was there.'

Many ghost stories are never fully explained and I suspect that this strange incident, and the identification of this haunting, will remain a mystery. However, what did strike me at the time I was informed of this encounter was the situation in which it was experienced – renovation – which I find is often the catalyst for stirring up the shades of the past that might otherwise lie dormant.

OLD LANGHO
THE BLACK BULL INN

Dating from the early 1550s, the Black Bull became a coaching inn on the main route between Whalley and Preston. It is infamous as a haunted hostelry and its main ghost story dates from 1648 when William Dutton, a member of Charles I's Royalist forces, became partial to the fare offered at the inn and also, it seems, to a serving wench named Elizabeth Fry. One evening, legend has it, he overstepped the mark with the serving maid, much to the annoyance of one Thomas Boves who had an arrangement regarding the favours of the young lady. He settled the matter in an ungentlemanly fashion by dispatching Mr Dutton with an agricultural implement!

In time honoured tradition the ghost of William Dutton walks the inn to this day, focussing particularly on the area where he met his gruesome end – now the restaurant. Staff past and present have encountered this phantom and appease him by setting an extra place in the dining room every night.

Perhaps we should forgive the ghost his misgivings of the past though, for it seems he saved a young child from badly

The Black Bull Inn.

hurting herself in recent years. Landlady Pam Morrell told me that a couple were coming down the stairs when their young daughter slipped. She would have gone head first into the stone wall at the bottom, but something invisible caught her and placed her upright on the bottom step, right before their very eyes. But the ghostly pranks are more often of a mischievous nature, according to Pam. 'He pinches things like make-up and tweezers, and also once locked one of the staff in the cellar for a while. The door doesn't stick, and she thought we were playing tricks on her, but we weren't – we weren't anywhere near.'

When I took Veronica there for a meal one evening recently, without telling her where we were going, she took me to one side after we had eaten informing me that she had seen the spirit of a man who haunts the older parts of the building. His appearance was tall and slender and he was adorned with a black cloak, a large silver clasp and a black hat. Veronica felt that he was the unfortunate victim of unrequited love, which was connected to a young blonde serving maid who had worked there in times past. At the end of her description Veronica said that 'savagery' had put an end to the unfortunate situation and the haunting was the result.

I couldn't argue with that!

The Black Bull Inn
Old Langho, Blackburn, BB6 8AW
Telephone: 01254 248801

OLDHAM
THE COLISEUM THEATRE

This theatre in Oldham, which dates back to 1887, is renowned for its well-attested ghost story. It has its roots in a tragic accident that occurred during a performance of *The Scottish Play* in January 1947. During a routine fight scene, actor Harold Norman was accidentally stabbed and subsequently died at Oldham hospital four weeks later. He was pronounced dead on 27th February – cause of death: peritonitis.

Having been struck down in his prime and without warning his spirit still lingers at the place where he played his final act. Noticed primarily as an unexplainable cold draught, his manifestations have mostly occurred on Thursdays, the day upon which he died.

When I contacted the theatre recently to see if they had anything new to report, I was informed that the ghost of Harold is still very much 'active' and that his performances still frighten theatre staff and workers alike.

Oldham Coliseum Theatre
Fairbottom Street, Oldham, OL1 3SW
Telephone:0161 624 1731
www.coliseum.org.uk

RUFFORD
RUFFORD OLD HALL

Rufford Old Hall, an elegant timber-framed mansion, was built for Sir Robert Hesketh around 1530 and sits quietly in a park of beech trees close to the town of Ormskirk. Claiming an interesting past, the house has played host to visiting dignitaries, including Queen Elizabeth I and William Shakespeare, who performed here in 1585. The baronial seat of the Heskeths, one of Lancashire's wealthiest families, for many centuries, it is now owned by the National Trust, who open the building to visitors between March and October. Its serene present day surroundings emit a calm and quiet atmosphere but it is an atmosphere that may be interrupted at any moment by one of its three resident ghosts.

The first spirit said to glide along the corridors of the older parts of the Hall is believed to be that of Elizabeth I herself. Recognisable from her portraits and opulent dress, she has been watched by astonished onlookers standing in the dining room apparently oblivious to those espying her. When approached, she simply fades away.

Rufford Old Hall.

Rufford's second shade is a more ambulatory spirit – the Grey Lady. It is thought she is the restless wraith of Elizabeth Hesketh, betrothed to an early Hesketh lord who was called to fight against the Scots on the eve of their wedding day; he never returned. Unable to accept his fate, she is alleged to have vowed never to remove the bridal gown until he returned, wandering hopelessly along the driveway and around the Hall in a desperate state of melancholy. She refused food and finally succumbed to her own sad fate by starvation. Years later she is still wandering here, although her dress is now described as tattered and grey.

Our last phantom at historic Rufford is that of an Elizabethan gentleman who has been sighted near the impressive fireplace in the Great Hall. His identity remains unknown but it has been suggested that he may be connected to the

'Secret Chamber', which was discovered high in the canopy above; a former hiding place for priests during the times of Catholic intolerance in the 16th century.

Rufford Old Hall
Rufford, near Ormskirk, L40 1SG
Telephone: 01704 821254

SALFORD
ORDSALL HALL

T he earliest record of the ancient manor house, known as Ordsall Hall, dates back to 1251 when William de Ferrers, Earl of Derby, exchanged the manor for land in Pendleton. However, it is most closely associated

Ordsall Hall.

with the Radclyffes who resided here for over 300 years. The family has a colourful history with inter-marriages, knighthoods and positions of influence each taking place at Ordsall. Famous Radclyffes include Sir Alexander who died in 1549 and was, on four occasions, High Sheriff of Lancashire, and Margaret Radclyffe, who died in 1599 and was a favourite maid of honour to Queen Elizabeth I.

During recent centuries more chapters have been added to the legacy of Ordsall Hall, including its use as a working men's club, a clergy training school, a family home and a church hall. In 1959 it was acquired by Salford City Council and an extensive long-term restoration programme was initiated before it was reopened in 1972. Today the council welcomes the public to enjoy the living history on offer, but many visitors go away not only with memories of the house itself, but also of its many ghostly inhabitants.

Ordsall's most famous phantom is that of the White Lady whose appearances tend to occur in the grand timber-framed Great Hall. Sightings of this ghost can be traced back over 70 years and she is the most frequently experienced spirit in the house. Her identity is a matter of speculation but rumour has it that she is the restless wraith of Lady Margaret Radclyffe, whose beloved brother was tragically killed during battle in Ireland. So bereft was Lady Margaret by this turn of events that she lost all appetite for life and indeed for food, which never again passed her lips. As a valued lady in waiting to the Queen herself, many luxurious delicacies were sent to Ordsall to tempt her palette, but to no avail. She died and was given a state burial before being interred in Westminster Abbey. It is said that her ghost still walks here in torment, seeking once again a brother whom she loved so dearly in life, and whom she continues to mourn even beyond death.

When Veronica and I visited Ordsall we were welcomed with great enthusiasm by the friendly staff. Each had their own ghostly encounters to relate. Museum curator Sam Smith has a wealth of information regarding strange sightings both inside the Hall and in the grounds. Whilst Veronica wandered around the grounds, Sam furnished me with the following tale of an incredible relationship shared by two sisters and the White Lady during the 1930s

'We had two wonderful old ladies visit the Hall in 2003; they were sisters and had lived here as children. They told me that their most vivid memory was of Celery – a woman whom they used to play with in the Great Hall. They recalled with absolute clarity that one of them could see Celery and the other could hear her. As adults they had often discussed this spectral playmate whom they remembered with fond affection and had assumed that they had misunderstood her name and that it was probably either Cecily or Cecile. They also remembered an old man who used to sit in the Great Hall watching them, but he had never spoken to them as Celery did. During their visit we were all walking up the staircase near the front door when suddenly they stopped in their tracks and looked at each other. "She's here," one said to the other. "Yes, I can feel her," the other replied, at which point a plastic light cover fell down and smashed, narrowly missing me. The ladies apologised profusely saying that it was just Celery saying "Hello" – apparently she always used to drop things in order to signify her presence to the ladies as children.'

Veronica joined me and we went into the Great Hall to see if she was able to contact the White Lady and verify her first name as either Margaret or Cecile/Cecily. Without prior knowledge she told me that there was a strong female entity in the room, a young spirit who 'flies' around and wears a 'strange hat and a long flowing dress'. Sam corroborated this and told us that Margaret Radclyffe, being the Queen's favourite maid of honour, had been given a very expensive dress costing £180 – an incredible amount of money for the 16th century. She continued by telling us that she felt the spirit made cyclical appearances and at times would go 'into hiding'. Veronica also felt that she would occasionally create a spectral scent to announce her presence, which was confirmed by Sam who said visitors had experienced a number of inexplicable smells in various parts of the building, which they had blamed on ghostly activity.

Sam elaborated on what she had already told me about this melancholic ghost with a story related to her by a friend. 'I was telling my friend that I was about to begin a job at Ordsall Hall when her face turned pale and she looked terrified. Asking her what was the matter, she told me that I should stay away from the place because it was haunted. She went on to explain that as a child she had been playing in the grounds of the Hall and had watched a strange woman through one of the windows who proceeded to walk through a wall and into the grounds, causing her to flee in terror. Despite this encounter being over 50 years ago she related it with the same freshness as if it had happened only yesterday, and she was clearly still severely affected by the memory.'

Leaving the Great Hall behind, we entered the Star Chamber, which takes its name from the wonderful hand-painted ceiling, featuring a star-filled night of deep azure blue and shining gold. The room is well known by staff as one of the haunted areas and Veronica walked across the room towards the bed, where she felt she could tune in best. After a few moments she told us she could sense the presence of another female spirit, but that this one was 'pushed aside' by the White Lady. The gentle shade was that of an elderly woman dressed in a blue gown. She was sitting at a loom frame and was connected with embroidery and tapestry work. She was neither happy nor sad, Veronica told us, 'She accepts her lot, and is a member of a family who once used this room, although not as a bedroom. There are small blue bottles associated with her, medicinal tinctures and books. This lady was suffering in this room and was treated here.' Sam said that various accounts of sweet medicinal smells in the room have been reported and that, as a part of the earliest building on the site, it had not always been in use as a bedchamber. Maybe the spectral scents are a reminder of the suffering this lady felt here so many years ago? We were about to leave the Star Chamber when Veronica told us there was someone else there. Sam's eyes widened with interest. 'Yes, you're right,' she said, 'I have had another encounter in this room. Can you ask the spirit to confirm what happened?'

Now this was a turn-up for the books! Usually I ask the living to confirm information allegedly received from the dead, but here Sam was asking the dead to confirm through Veronica what she had experienced. Veronica's eyes were tightly shut. 'It is a man; he is smoking a pipe with tobacco mixed with leaves,' she said, and then she did something I have never seen her do in all the years I have known her, she spoke in the first person in a deep voice: 'I smelt of horses.' Sam almost jumped for joy. 'Yes,' she shrieked, unable to contain her amazement. Three years before, Sam had encountered a pungent smell of rotten manure in this room; it lasted over ten minutes and then dissipated and had never returned.

I found this amazing; not only had the correct information been related by the spirit through Veronica but it also indicated that the spirit was aware of our presence and of Sam's question – answering directly in the first person through the medium! By this time Veronica was considerably tired and we decided to go to Sam's office for a rest, but the ghosts were not finished yet.

As we climbed the main staircase to the Tudor Upper Gallery area, Veronica was gripped by the presence of a fourth ghost. It was a tall male spirit, which she described as wearing ritual robes and a large bloodstone ring and having long black hair and a pointed beard. Perhaps it was a Freemason or member of the order of the Knights Templar? Veronica found him 'secretive and covering himself in a large cloak so I cannot see him fully' and said he was pacing vigorously up and down the gallery. This was corroborated by Sam as many people had reported loud heavy footsteps there, which they had presumed belonged to a male. She had experienced this spirit herself, having felt him breathing on her neck from behind; she had also heard knocking on her office door when there was no one else in the building.

After we had enjoyed a short rest and a well-earned cup of coffee, Sam invited us to visit some areas of the Hall dating from the 14th century, which were

The Star Chamber.

undergoing restoration and were not open to the public. First up was the Solar in which Veronica said she was aware of religious conflict. Sam validated this by telling us that the room was once a chapel and that despite being a Royalist household during times of Catholic persecution, the occupants were allowed to continue practising the Catholic faith by paying heavily for the privilege instead of obeying new laws dictating they must become Protestant. Footsteps in this room have also been heard from the Star Chamber below, even though access doors have been locked and there have been no conservation staff on duty at the time.

In the Plaster Ceiling Room Sam told us that a strange ephemeral light has been seen in the corner by the large stone fireplace in the peripheral vision of percipients. However, when stared at, there is nothing to be seen. Kerry Atkinson is a member of staff at the Hall and has encountered two of the building's ghosts, the first in this room. She told me, 'I was alone at the time, going about my work, tidying up the room to prepare it for building work, when suddenly I had the impression that I was not alone. It was that kind of flesh creeping sensation you get when you feel threatened and, in my mind, I sensed that it was the spirit of a woman who did not want me there. I ran out of the room and I have not been back since.' Hours later the same day, Kerry had another experience, this time in the Star Chamber: 'I was vacuuming the carpet on which the visitors walk when out of the corner of my eye I saw a hovering egg-shaped yellow light. As I watched, it moved quickly and silently along the ground, around my legs and disappeared. In my mind I felt that this was the same woman that I had experienced in the Plaster Ceiling Room – but that this time she was happy for me to be with her. It was a day I will never forget!'

We left Ordsall Hall content in the knowledge that we had visited one of the most haunted houses in Lancashire, and had been fortunate enough to not only sense the presence of ghosts, but also speak directly to a spirit beyond the grave.

Keen ghost hunters can gain virtual access to Ordsall Hall's most haunted areas online via two web based 'Ghost Cams' installed by the council to increase interest in the Hall. I was asked to figurehead the launch of their second camera in the Star Chamber in October 2005 and I will be keeping a close eye on any evidence of the paranormal this captures. Please do let me know if you spot anything.

Ordsall Hall
Ordsall Lane, Ordsall, Salford, Manchester, M5 3AN
Telephone: 0161 872 0251
www.salford.gov.uk/museums

TURTON
TURTON TOWER

Beyond an imposing gatehouse, at the end of a long drive, stands an eccentric's dream, Turton Tower. Originally constructed in 1420, the tower has evolved over five centuries into an impressive country house,

Turton Tower.

which is now open to the public. At its heart, a medieval stone pele tower reaches for the skies and a variety of timber-framed additions cling to its ivy-clad walls, creating a unique and motley appearance akin to something from the pages of Sir Arthur Conan Doyle.

The tower is reputedly haunted by an unidentified woman in a black gown who ascends a spiral staircase in the oldest part of the building and floats silently across a chamber before disappearing down a former garderobe (privy). Another room houses an old wooden cradle that has been seen rocking of its own volition and, on occasions, loud banging has been heard throughout the house, with no apparent natural explanation.

A more contemporary account tells of three teenagers who watched what they described as 'an Elizabethan ghost' walk past them while they were visiting the building; they were so alarmed by their sighting that none told their respective parents until years later. I was keen to see if Veronica could uncover any new ghosts in this old haunt.

There is a strange magic in old houses that have been shut away from prying eyes and this was evident as Veronica and I were shown into the dark oak-panelled library early one crisp autumn morning. Our guide, Robert Orrell, had unlocked the door and we crossed the threshold before turning to look at each other – this room had 'that' feeling.

By 'that' feeling I mean an intangible but distinct atmosphere that is somehow different from normal. Of course Veronica is used to this experience as part of her work as a medium but, on this occasion, even I could feel the sense of haunting, oozing from the very walls around us. In the corner, a suit of armour stared as we moved around the chamber, absorbing the strange sensation and trying to make sense of it.

I powered up the ghost radar, a kind of portable sensing device that picks up unusual changes in the temperature, electromagnetic energy, movements and biometrics of the human body. The red flashing indicator light temporarily quashed the gloom and sent the shadows fleeing into the fireplace as I tried to capture evidence of something supernatural among us. Veronica started to perceive a male and female with a strong attachment to the house but she was sure that they were not in this room. 'We need to go further up,' she stated suddenly. So we left the haunted library and were shown into the dining room.

'I am drawn to this painting,' Veronica said, indicating a portrait of a dour-faced man. 'That's Oliver Cromwell,' Robert informed us. Veronica continued with her psychic investigation, telling me that she felt he had a strong connection with the building. Suddenly a loud beeping alerted us to a possible presence via the ghost radar, which was flashing madly. Veronica told us that she could hear marching feet, and Robert explained that Cromwell's troops had been entertained at Turton during the Civil War.

With our initial success we decided to leave Oliver Cromwell behind and explore the building further. We climbed the winding staircase to the first floor and made for the drawing room. As soon as we entered, Veronica was seeing images in her mind. 'This room is full of ladies holding fans. Poetry, music and a piano have had a place in this room in the past.' Robert verified her vision by telling us that in the Turton archives several photographs taken during the Victorian era show ladies and children sitting around a grand piano in this room.

'There is another spirit here, though,' Veronica continued. 'He is pacing up and down and I feel he is waiting for an important letter or document. He is wearing a frilly shirt and a leather waistcoat and I see him searching through a wooden chest as if he has lost something. He is in great danger and his emotion is one of fear. I think he is going to flee.' I asked Veronica if he was aware of the ladies and the piano, but she told me he was from a different and much earlier time, which made sense later when I examined the layout of the building as the drawing room is in the earliest section which dates back to the medieval period.

On our way up to the next floor we stopped in the Tapestry Bedroom which Veronica felt had been used by servants. 'Correct again' said Robert, telling us that the room had indeed once been a servants' room.

We had already experienced a plethora of psychic evidence and a reaction on the ghost radar but it wasn't until we went into the Chetham Room in the highest part of the tower that we met with our most incredible experience at Turton.

The room is named after the Chetham family who bought Turton Tower in 1648. It is now sparsely furnished and used as a display gallery for local arts and crafts. It is not unfair to say that this is the plainest chamber in the building and therefore contains no visual clues as to its past. Veronica went over to a small window in the far corner of the room where she became aware of a man with long hair and a pointed nose looking out of the window. He was watching children playing outside but he was not happy. He showed Veronica a large leather-bound bible and two chalices, which were empty. 'The emptiness is somehow important,' she told us.

Robert had left us at this point to attend to his duties elsewhere in the house and so I scribbled down Veronica's statements and we made our way back down the wooden stairs to meet up with him in the hall. I told him what Veronica had sensed in the Chetham Room and that she was convinced that the chalices had great significance. He paused and gave us a strange look before smiling and delivering a startling revelation, which was so precise in its verification that even I was surprised.

'There is a very old tale associated with two human skulls that are hidden away under lock and key in this house,' he began. 'The skulls are those of a man and woman, and they were found in Bradshaw Brook in 1750. They were taken to a farm, which no longer exists, at Timberbottom where they were kept as curiosities. From that time on, any attempt to move the grisly artefacts brought havoc to the house, including unexplained blood-curdling screams, moving furniture and loud banging. Years later, in 1840, a farm tenant arranged to have them buried in Bradshaw churchyard but this did not silence the skulls whose manifestations were so violent that they were soon dug up and returned to their place on the mantelpiece at Timberbottom. Only the demolition of the farmhouse could persuade the skulls to accept a new home and they were moved to Bradshaw Hall, itself pulled down in the 1950s. They were then presented to Turton Tower by our benefactor, Colonel Hardcastle.' He then turned to Veronica and said, 'The remarkable thing is that the skulls are so ancient that the two pieces that still remain of them are the skull caps, which closely resemble cups or chalices, and they were actually displayed here for many years, on top of a large bible in the Chetham Room.'

Amazed by the accuracy of the evidence supplied by Veronica, we were keen to see the Timberbottom Skulls but our request was refused by the curator who told me that they were securely hidden away in some attic in the house and that she didn't know their exact location. As we left Turton Tower, I glanced at my notes from the visit and I wondered if the male and female that Veronica had sensed in the library, when we first arrived, could have been the sentient incarnations of the skulls.

It is sad to think that after centuries of respect at Timberbottom Farm and Bradshaw Hall the skulls of these two unfortunates are now gathering dust behind several locked doors at Turton Tower. Perhaps they should instigate their poltergeist manifestations once again as they have done in the past.

Turton Tower
Chapeltown Road, Turton, near Bolton, BL7 OHG
Telephone: 01204 852203

WHALLEY
WHALLEY ABBEY

The once grand abbey at Whalley was founded in Stanlow, Cheshire. It moved to Whalley in 1296, where it flourished until the Dissolution of the Monasteries in 1537, following the orders of King Henry VIII. It is now a romantic ruin and whispers of times past still linger in phantom form.

Encounters with ghostly monks in the ruins date back to the 1960s and include the sound of chanting and sightings of robed figures, which have also been caught on film. In addition, a curious experience has been reported by one lady who, whilst sitting on a bench, felt a reassuring hand placed on her shoulder even though there was no one around. Ghostly goings on at Whalley are attributed to the spirit of Abbot John Paslew, the last abbot here, whose 'fighting spirit' during life is noted in many accounts of the troubles here in 1537.

Whalley Abbey.

When I visited the Abbey with Veronica, it was a warm serene afternoon. As the only visitors there at the time, we were easily lost in the ethereal atmosphere of its ruins. 'There are two distinctly different vibrations here,' Veronica claimed. 'On one side there is great disharmony and conflict, this is a memory of things past, but the spirit is that of a hooded man.' We both found ourselves smiling at the cliché – we were in a ruined abbey after all! Nevertheless this gave some credence to the tale of Abbot Paslew's haunting.

In the kitchen area, Veronica sensed a female spirit whom she perceived to be part of a Georgian family who had lived at the Abbey. Unbeknown to her, part of the Abbey, now known as Assheton House, became a residence in Elizabethan times and remained in private hands until 1923 when the Church of England acquired it. Veronica identified the spirit as a distressed lady whom she felt had lost a child. She was accompanied by a whippet dog and was pacing up and down.

I decided to take Veronica to the north-west gatehouse, which is separated from the ruins by a short walk. 'I feel this is a place of worship, not merely a gatehouse,' Veronica said. As we left this haunting place and walked back to the car, I revealed to her that the gatehouse did indeed house a chapel on its first floor!

Whalley Abbey
Whalley, Clitheroe, BB7 9SS
Telephone: 01254 822268
www.whalleyabbey.co.uk

WORSLEY
WARDLEY HALL

The grisly relic of a disturbed past lies hidden behind a secret panel at Wardley Hall, home of the Roman Catholic Bishop of Salford.

The 'Screaming Skull', as it has become known, has a mysterious heritage and was thought at one time to have been the bony remains of Royalist, Roger Downs, who was killed during a brawl on Tower Bridge in London.

Locally, however, it is now accepted that the skull is that of a former Benedictine monk named Father Ambrose who, on 10th September 1641, at the age of 56, was hung, drawn and quartered in brutal fashion after professing his Catholic faith under a Protestant state, for which he was made a saint in 1970. After his death the head was paraded on show in Manchester as an example to those who might follow in his footsteps. It was later retrieved by a Catholic sympathiser named Francis Downe, who concealed the head in a wall of his Tudor home, Wardley Hall, where it remained undisturbed until it was discovered by a later owner, Matthew Morton, in 1745 – a century after Father Ambrose's unfortunate demise.

Morton decided the gruesome find would best be kept hidden from prying eyes, and so it was returned to its place of rest. But the skull, whose power had lain dormant for so many years, was about to invoke a terrible toll.

Ownership of the Hall soon passed to a new landlord, who brought with him a small army of servants. It wasn't long before the skull's hiding place was discovered and the ugly treasure it entombed was carelessly thrown into the moat surrounding the Hall. That night a violent storm, the like of which had not been seen in decades, ripped through the skies at Wardley. Screams of a tormented soul rang through the chambers of the manor, as if the skull was venting a terrible wrath on those who had discarded it so foolishly. In a state of panic the moat was dredged and the skull was returned to its rightful resting place, after which the storms relented and the screams were no more.

Many quiet years passed and the tormented spirit attached to the skull held its silence in the wall at Wardley until one night in 1930, when a thief broke into the mansion and took, amongst other priceless items, the famed haunted skull. Once again, all hell broke out in the area; storms ravaged local houses and powerful winds uprooted trees around the Hall. The violence continued unabated for several nights until late one evening there was a tapping at a window. Bishop Thomas Henshaw, then incumbent at Wardley, opened the window to find a terrified local shaking with fear and grasping an old hessian sack, which he thrust into the bishop's hands before disappearing into the dark night. When he unravelled the sack, the grinning skull of Father Ambrose stared up at the bishop, and peace returned once more to Wardley.

In the technologically-advanced world in which we live, it is interesting to note that a modern clause was entered into the lease of the Hall stating that the skull may not be removed from the premises under any circumstances!

WYCOLLER

One of Lancashire's hidden gems is undoubtedly the picturesque and mysterious village of Wycoller, which can be accessed only on foot, unless you are a resident. I have been lucky enough to spend much time here, especially in my childhood when family friends owned a farmhouse at the very centre of the hamlet.

It was a beautiful summer afternoon when Veronica and I strolled down the path into the village not long ago and, as the way became narrower and the trees met overhead creating a lush green canopy of shadow, it was as if we were walking backward in time itself.

Running through the centre of the village is a babbling brook that glistens in the sunlight and casts a magical light show on the ancient stones of 16th-century Wycoller Hall, which lies ruined, a crumbling skeleton of its former self. The hauntings at Wycoller are well documented and have been witnessed in recent years by residents and visiting tourists alike. The most prevalent is the

The ruins of Wycoller Hall.

spectacular phantom horseman, Squire Cunliffe, who gallops into the village before entering the Hall amidst blood curdling screams, said to be those of his wife whom he brutally murdered by beating her to death with a dog whip after finding her in the arms of another.

The second ghost, locally known as the Black Lady, has migrated from the confines of the Hall ruins and now haunts the entire surrounding area, particularly favouring the packhorse bridge, which crosses the beck. Dressed from top to toe in black silk and of West Indian descent, she has been seen by many visitors in recent years, often startling them with her sudden unannounced presence. She is thought to have been murdered by her husband, who had second thoughts after marrying her during a trip to the West Indies and threw her overboard, and she mournfully lingers still at the place she never called home.

The third spectre of Wycoller is that of a phantom coach and horses, which clatters through the village on dark moonlit nights when the wind howls and the rain pelts down upon the cottages. Although this phenomenon is thought by many to be merely a legend, I was interested to find a first-hand account in a book by author Terence Whitaker. It tells of a young couple who visited the village late one night, parking on the verge next to the Hall. They were disturbed by a loud noise, which they described like 'dragging chains across the car roof'. After getting out of the car to investigate, they were unable to find an explanation for the sound, which by now had begun again, only this time much louder. Deciding it would be best if

Sally's Bridge, Wycoller.

they left, they tried to start the engine but it failed to turn over. By now the temperature in the car had plummeted and they could clearly see their breath, which was becoming much faster! In a state of panic they tried again to start the car as a thunderous calamity of sound seemed to pass right through them and the car itself. It wasn't until the sound had faded away that the car jumped into action and they sped out of Wycoller, never to return.

When I took Veronica across the packhorse bridge, also known as Sally's Bridge after the woman who was responsible for having it built, she stopped in her tracks. Looking back at the arches, she said, 'There's a lady in a black dress following us across the bridge. She has a sombre frame of mind and I think she may have committed suicide.' I wondered whether the unhappy West Indian bride had indeed taken her own life and that popular legend was in fact incorrect? There were other faint psychic memories among the ruins, including a shrouded figure laid out following death inside the Hall and two men fighting a duel, but nothing as strong as the sense of the Black Lady, and no trace of Squire Cunliffe atop his spectral steed or the terrifying clatter of the coach and horses.

When I returned to my office I came across a report by some local psychic investigators who investigated the ruins in 1996. They claim to have recorded a sound that they heard at the time and described as 'similar to a riding crop' – could this have been a psychic echo of the dog whip used by Squire Cunliffe to murder his wife centuries earlier?

The colourful history of Wycoller and its haunted heritage mostly eluded us that summer day, but there can be no doubt that events have taken place there that have left a powerful psychic footprint on the atmosphere – so much so that their emanations can still be sensed many hundreds of years later.

•Acknowledgements•

I must thank the psychic mediums, Veronica Charles, Sybil Lucas-Brewer and Angela Borrows and also Wendy Craig and Sian Rayner for arranging visits to the locations featured in this book. Thanks also to those at the featured locations, in particular:

Liz at Hall i' th' Wood

Elizabeth Tatman at Smithills Hall

Ken Darwen & Christine Howard at Towneley Hall

Brian Watson for the account of his experience in the grounds of Towneley Hall

Steve & Jeanne at the Sun Inn, Chipping

Claire Rowbotham and Robert Gregg at the Dunkenhalgh Hotel

Robert Redmayne Parker at Browsholme Hall

Elda & Raymond Lempereur, Rita Jackson and Neil Bascombe of Croxteth Hall

Vicky Davies & Kerri Richards at Marley's Winebar, Darwen

Barry Shepherd at the New Inn, Foulridge

Ian at Haigh Hall

Susan Burke at the Punch Bowl Inn, Hurst Green

Adele & Roger Yeomans at Mains Hall

Lord Nick & Lady Eva Speakman at Stubley Hall

Norman Wolstencroft of Tonge Hall

Sam Smith and Kerry Atkinson at Ordsall Hall

Robert Orrell at Turton Tower

Colin Veacock for his report on Wycoller Hall

Liz Smith for her account of her encounter at Bygone Times

Charlie Bowman at the Inn at Whitewell

Finally, Tony Ortzen, Paul Brett and Rebecca Weller at *Psychic News*, Amanda Griffiths at *Lancashire Life* and Carole Turner at BBC Radio Lancashire.

•Bibliography•

Armand, Muriel *The Ghosts of Lancashire* Print Origination, 1993

Eyre, Kathleen *Lancashire Ghosts* Dalesman, 1989

Hassall, Keith & Firth, Mike *Haunted Halls of Lancashire* Lancashire Books, 1990

Hough, Peter *Supernatural Lancashire* Hale, 2003

Howarth, Ken Ghosts, *Traditions & Legends of Old Lancashire* Sigma Leisure, 1993

Quinlan, Janette & McGrath, Shaun *Haunted Sites of Oldham* Oldham Education & Leisure, 1999

Warren, Melanie & Wells, Tony *Ghosts of the North* Broadcast Books, 1995

Whitaker, Terence *Lancashire's Ghosts & Legends*, Granada, 1982

Whitaker, Terence *North Country Ghosts & Legends*, Grafton Books, 1988

Underwood, Peter *Ghosts of North West England*, Fontana, 1978

•Index•